HOW TO TELL IF YOUR KIDS ARE USING DRUGS

HOW TO TELL IF YOUR KIDS ARE USING DRUGS

Timothy Dimoff and Steve Carper

Facts On File

New York • Oxford

How to Tell If Your Kids Are Using Drugs

Facts On File, Inc.   Facts On File Limited
460 Park Avenue South   Collins Street
New York NY 10016   Oxford OX4 1XJ
USA   United Kingdom

Library of Congress Cataloging-in-Publication Data
Dimoff, Timothy.
    How to tell if your kids are using drugs / Timothy Dimoff and Steve Carper.
        p. cm.
    Includes index.
    ISBN 0-8160-2473-1 (alk. paper)
      1. Children—United States—Drug use.   2. Teenagers—United States—Drug use.   3. Children—United States—Alcohol use.   4. Teenagers—United States—Alcohol use.   I. Carper, Steve.   II. Title.
HV5824.C45D56   1991
649'.4—dc20   91-15103

A British CIP catalogue record for this book is available from the British Library.

Facts On File books are available at special discounts when purchased in bulk quantities for businesses, associations, institutions or sales promotions. Please contact our Special Sales Department in New York at 212/683-2244 (dial 800/322-8755 except in NY, AK, or HI) or in Oxford at 865/728399.

Text design by Ron Monteleone
Jacket design by James Victore
Composition by Facts On File, Inc.
Manufactured by the Maple-Vail Manufacturing Group
Printed in the United States of America

10 9 8 7 6 5 4 3 2 1

This book is printed on acid-free paper.

To all parents who have already experienced the pain and sorrow of knowing that their sons or daughters have been involved with the abuse of alcohol or other drugs.

Contents

Acknowledgments

We would like to extend our appreciation to Karen Greenawalt, a certified drug counselor and a cherished friend. Her invaluable advice and contributions to the development of this book cannot go without special acknowledgment.

1

Children and Drugs in America: Welcome to the 1990s

Have your children tried drugs?
In all likelihood, yes.

What more needs to be said about children and drugs in today's America? Without knowing you, without ever meeting your children, we can say that by the time they are seniors in high school they have probably already smoked, drunk, snorted or injected a drug—at least one drug, probably more. They may have procured it easily and cheaply, at a cost no more than that of a CD or a deluxe pizza. More likely they received a free taste of something being passed around at a party, or from a buddy in a car on a Saturday night or—most common and saddest of all—from the store of drugs you have casually displayed in your home, the ones you use in front of them.

As parents, you should know—must know—whether your children have continued to use alcohol or other drugs after their first experimentation, whether they are regularly using these drugs even today, whether drugs could be the cause of their lowered grades in school or loss of interest in sports or the air of general hostility around the house.

You should know, but you probably don't. Despite all the talk about the alcohol and drug problem in this country, most parents still refuse to believe that their own children may be involved. Many of you reading this book will be amazed, possibly even offended, that we opened this chapter by saying flatly that your children have probably experimented with drugs. Parents are the last to know. Look at these statistics from a recent Lewis Harris poll:

▼   36% of parents surveyed thought their children had taken a drink; 66% of students surveyed said they had.

▼   14% of parents thought their children had tried cigarettes; 41% of the students said they had.

▼   5% of parents thought their children had used illicit drugs; 17% of the students said they had.

You don't know, but you should.

The best way for you to tell if your children are doing drugs is to become knowledgeable about the world of drugs yourself. That's the purpose of this book.

In this chapter and in the two that follow we'll provide facts and figures on the true amount of drug use by youth in this country; explain to you the various stages of experimentation, use or abuse that children may be in; and tie these stages into detailed information about the workings and appearances of the many different drugs that kids are known to use. We'll also offer insights into the major reasons why kids try drugs in the first place and suggest explanations of how and why children get away with their drug use.

These chapters should provide you with the context you will need to properly evaluate the heart of this book—some 200 warning signs of possible drug use or abuse, which we call Red Flags. We hope that you will study the Red Flags carefully and with open, objective—and, by that point, better educated—minds. Please remember that other problems may be bound up with drug use or may mimic the symptoms of use even when drugs are not present. Getting help for an ailing child should be your objective, whatever the cause might be.

If you decide that the evidence of the Red Flags is such that you must confront your child about drug use, we end with an extremely critical chapter giving you suggestions on how to conduct that confrontation and, just as important, how to set up a drug-free home atmosphere for the entire family.

Along the way you'll also see sections in which the editorial "we" is dropped and Tim Dimoff steps out and speaks directly to you from his years of experience as a former narcotics officer with the Akron Police Department. These will often not make pleasant reading, but they are designed to show graphically why it is so important for you to become actively involved if you suspect your child is abusing drugs.

Before we start, we need to define some terms so that we can be sure you are thinking along the same lines that we are.

One thing we hope to show you is that the regular use of any one drug leads to the use of others. That first drug, the one that opens the gate to further use, is naturally called a "gateway drug." Most people are under the impression that drugs are always illegal. This is not always the case. In fact, most gateway drugs are not illegal at all.

You know the names of these drugs because you may use them yourselves. One is tobacco, a deadly long-term killer for those who get hooked while young. The other is the worst, most used, most abused, most deadly drug our children lay their hands on: alcohol. Because in our society they are legal products for adults, tobacco and alcohol are sometimes placed in a category separate from the proscribed drugs. Those other substances are then collectively referred to as "illicit" drugs. We will keep that distinction in this book. Please remember, though, that for youth, alcohol and tobacco products are just as illicit as any other drug.

When parents think about drugs, they too often think only about the illicit drugs. This is a huge mistake. Many of the symptoms, behaviors and problems we'll talk about are more likely to come from alcohol than from any of the other drugs. Unfortunately, *drug* is too common a word and embedded in too many common phrases not to use. Sometimes we'll say specifically "alcohol and other drugs." Even when we don't, even when for convenience we just use the word *drug*, we want you to always think of alcohol as well.

You have the final responsibility for identifying whether your child is currently using alcohol and other drugs. Teachers, clergy, counselors and others don't have the time or opportunity to see your children the way you do. Our hope is that by educating you about the world of drugs and children in today's America, you'll be able to make that identification for yourself.

To start with: How did we ever get in a state where it is necessary for parents to make these decisions about their children? Perhaps we should have known: When it comes to drugs, America has been there before.

America: A Drug-Laden History

Drugs have always been a part of American culture, just as they have been in virtually every society throughout history. Tobacco, of course, is a New World discovery, and pipes, cigars and snuff were found in almost every home. Our ancestors also swilled down casks of wine, beer, whiskey and homemade hooch. Although temperance waves stormed through the country, first as a religious force in the 1840s and then as a political movement

3

in the 1870s, neither one stopped drinking; the movements merely made it sufficiently disreputable that it had to reemerge in a more respectable form. Patent medicines evolved as a licit way to make Americans of the late 19th century feel good. Fortified by the tremendous alcohol content in these concoctions, Americans never had to set foot in a saloon to get drunk. And if alcohol wasn't enough of a kick, our grandfathers could try a cocaine cigar while our grandmothers could delicately sip cocaine tea.

Shocked by the resulting addictions, legislators, backed by muckraking newspaper campaigns, passed a series of laws attacking cocaine, heroin and opium. Finally, alcohol remained as the last and biggest target. When the 18th Amendment and the Volstead Act made the manufacture and sale of alcoholic beverages illegal in 1919, most Americans thought they had won a major victory over the problem of alcoholism. Instead, the Roaring Twenties brought gangsters, speakeasies and a new generation hooked on booze.

Attitudes toward drugs have radically shifted several times in our history, but the feeling that drugs could be a powerful positive force rather than a menace reached its peak in the 1960s and 1970s. Despite endless scare stories in the media, a significant and vocal part of that college generation claimed to abandon alcohol and turned instead to marijuana and LSD for gentler, groovier highs. The decriminalization of marijuana was largely achieved in many states, and nationwide legalization was expected to soon follow.

Marijuana use became more the symbol of a generation than a crime. During the 1988 presidential campaign, candidates Albert Gore and Richard Babbitt admitted that they had smoked pot in college. Douglas Ginsberg was forced to withdraw his name as a nominee for the Supreme Court after he confirmed he had smoked marijuana, but the furor was over his use of the drug after college, as a professor. Thousands of other public figures have acknowledged smoking pot as well. Pot was established as an accepted generational rite.

In the 1970s, cocaine was also believed to be benign, nonaddictive, and, except perhaps for a few extreme users, not physically harmful. In 1973, in fact, a National Commission on Marijuana and Drug Abuse report said that little social cost related to cocaine had been verified in the United States. By the 1980s, the entire country understood how wrong that report had been.

Wars against substance abuse have often failed in America because too large a percentage of the country's adults were themselves using the very drugs that were the sources of abuse. Campaigns against drugs as varied as alcohol, marijuana, cocaine and Valium fell short because the drugs' dangers were not taken seriously by their users. Although reliable statistics are hard to come by, it is safe to say that by the latter half of the 1970s, as high a percentage of adult

Americans as we had ever seen used or condoned the use of the largest and most varied quantity of licit and illicit, doctor-approved or street-tested, drugs in our country's history. Americans truly believed in a pill for every ill.

The Drug Culture Retreats

From Prohibition to Repeal was only 14 years, but in those years American attitudes about alcohol nearly reversed. Historians will look back and note a similarly astounding turnaround over the past 14 years. During this time the drug culture has been hit with three major blows, blows so severe that even those most vocal about drug acceptance have begun to waver.

First came the gradual realization that all the terrible things some people had been saying about drugs for so long were true.

▼ Although the surgeon general first warned against cigarettes way back in 1964, an ever-widening series of medical studies have shown that smoking causes lung cancer, heart disease, emphysema and a host of other diseases. To breathe in other people's smoke is now known to be almost as bad as smoking itself.

▼ The dangers of alcohol were finally appreciated. Not only do alcoholics themselves suffer, but so do the fetuses of pregnant alcohol users and the children and spouses of alcoholics. Thousands of people kill themselves and others through alcohol- impaired driving, which finally has been perceived to be a preventable crime. Groups such as MADD (Mothers Against Drunk Driving) appeared in towns all over the country, and "designated driver" became a familiar phrase.

▼ Marijuana smoke may be free of tobacco's nicotine, but its tar and hundreds of other chemicals were shown to be similarly damaging to human lungs and to have the potential to cause other physical ills.[1]

▼ Cocaine use proved to be extremely addicting and also to lead to nasal and respiratory problems, paranoia and—unexpectedly and almost overnight—to a dramatic surge in deaths from cardiac arrest, respiratory failure or brain hemorrhage.[2]

---

[1] Donald Ian Macdonald, *Drugs, Drinking, and Adolescents* (Chicago: Year Book Medical Publishers, 1984), 55–67.

[2] Jesse E. Tarr and Martin Macklin, "Cocaine," *Pediatric Clinics of North America*, 34:2 (April 1982), 324.

For a population seemingly committed to a long-term campaign of health improvement through exercise, better food, lowered stress and closer attention to their bodies, the abuse of drugs was a contradiction many could no longer abide. Complete abstinence was rare, but a wave of moderation showed up in the form of light beers, trendy low-alcohol wines and drinks and ever-lower tar and nicotine cigarettes. Liquor and tobacco companies saw their overall growth slow, halt and then reverse for the first time in decades.

Second, drugs themselves changed. Homegrown marijuana in the 1960s was of such poor quality that hippies engaged in constant quests for foreign pot in the hopes of scoring a better high. Other drugs were of similarly low-potency. The average packet of cocaine was only 20% pure. Street heroin was cut so much by inert additives that it averaged only 6% of the drug.

While damage could surely be done by these low-voltage drugs—drug casualties abounded even during the 1960s and 1970s—the weaker drugs then taken meant that most highs were not as prolonged or as damaging and that addictions took more time to develop and were easier to break.

For whatever reasons, these street drugs never took a moderating route similar to their licit counterparts. Today's illicit drugs are as "new and improved" as any detergent or cake mix on supermarket shelves.

Consider these facts:

▼ Marijuana is 5 to 20 times stronger today than the average street drug of the sixties.[3]
▼ Cocaine can run as much as 80% pure drug.
▼ Street heroin now averages 14% pure drug and can be found 99% pure.[4]

Narcotics officers and emergency room staff know what a difference these vastly more powerful substances can make. The increase in the number of cocaine deaths can be measured in large part by the increased purity of the drug that, ironically, users pay a premium for. Knowledgeable users even made their drugs more potent at home by freebasing cocaine—using a solvent to separate any remaining impurities from the coke.

Rumors of the powerful highs achieved from these high-potency ultra-pure drugs filtered down into the street. Users who could not afford the

---

[3] United States Department of Education, *What Works: Schools Without Drugs* (1986): 9.
[4] U.S. *News and World Report*, July 28, 1986, p. 50.

premium drugs nevertheless wanted to get the same kicks. But their street drugs had often been cut—diluted—several times by dealers trying to bulk out the drugs. A kilogram of pure cocaine sold to one dealer in Florida can be mixed with as many as nine kilos of white powder by the time it hits the streets in the North.

Drug dealers are ruthless entrepreneurs. They figured out ways of putting back the kicks into their diluted drugs. Dealers dip marijuana cigarettes into formaldehyde to increase their potency and boost cocaine's power with speed (amphetamines) or even rat poison. More so than ever before, any drug sold on the street may be lethal either by being pure or by not being pure. It's a no-win proposition either way.

Worse, dealers then attach a fancy name to their poisons and can sell them for higher prices. Tim has often seen dealers pull these stunts during his work as an undercover narcotics officer:

> One dealer was having a lot of success near a school. Every day kids would line up to buy. I went to make a buy from him, told him I wanted to buy some smoke [marijuana]. He told me he didn't have any, but he had something better, "Gutchie Gutchie." He said it was a special blend direct from the South and he could only get it twice a year so it cost $10.00 more per bag. I was wired up with a body transmitter and I could picture in my mind the other backup detectives hidden down the street laughing and rolling on the ground. With a straight face I said I'd buy some. All Gutchie Gutchie turned out to be was marijuana with some chemicals on it, but the unique name with the story was all he needed to say to entice junior high school kids. The second time I went back he sold me "Double Gutchie Gutchie." I said this is it and arrested him. Gutchie Gutchie got him three years.

The rise of designer drugs, chemical variations of known drugs that are illicit drugs under current law, introduced even more risks. Designer drugs—a catchy name that law enforcement officials hate, since it makes the drugs seem chic and desirable—can produce almost any effect, can be of any potency and can just as easily be fatal. No studies are made of the drugs' effects; no one tries them on animals to screen out the more deadly ones. Users are acting as guinea pigs for the dealers. Only the survivors come back to buy again.

The third blow to our once-benign conception of drugs is in many ways the most deadly. In the past a legitimate argument could be made (and often was) that users of alcohol and other drugs were adults with the right to decide what to do with their own lives, even if that meant destroying them. The drug scene in the 1970s and 1980s changed all that. For the first time in our drug-laden history, adults weren't the only major consumers of drugs. Our children had joined us.

Children in the Drug World:
As Never Before

In 1982, the California Department of Education noted the contrast between the discipline problems in schools in 1940 and those of today. Half a century ago the problems were so mild as to seem part of an Andy Hardy movie: not putting paper in wastebaskets, making noise, running in the halls. The two most significant problems in public schools were, believe it or not, talking and chewing gum. Any more serious problems—which certainly existed—must have been seen as isolated and atypical.

Today there are no problems too bad not to make the list. The top two are ones not even dreamed of in an Andy Hardy nightmare: drug abuse and alcohol abuse. The rest of the list, which includes absenteeism, robbery and burglary, suicide, and gang warfare, would probably fade into 1940s-like isolation were they not caused by or worsened by drug and alcohol abuse. It is a very different world in schools today—junior high and elementary schools as well as high schools, private and parochial as well as public. Your memories of the "fast" kids in school sneaking a six-pack or a joint bear no resemblance to the realities of modern school life.

How bad is the situation today? A lot depends on how you want to read it. While there is plenty of discouraging news, there is much good as well. Most children are obviously not addicted to drugs. Teen groups (such as Students Against Drunk Driving) show that kids can be responsible and constructively address a bad situation.

Even so, as we said earlier, we know that virtually all children have tried drugs. And the use of the gateway drugs alone presents a tremendous health problem—current and future—to our children. Look at what the research has shown:

▼ There are an estimated 3 million adolescent alcoholics in this country.[5]

▼ Three out of every ten kids have tried alcohol by the time they finish the eighth grade and 17% have gotten drunk. Four out of ten have

---

[5] Macdonald, *Drugs, Drinking, and Adolescents*, 1.

tried cigarettes and 6% are smoking daily. One out of seven has used an illicit drug.[6]

▼ Someone who starts smoking before age 14 is fifteen times more likely to develop lung cancer than a non-smoker.

▼ If teens do not start smoking by the age of 21, they're not likely to do so afterward.

▼ Only one-quarter of fourth graders think that a wine cooler a day is harmful. Even fewer believe that wine coolers should be considered drugs.

▼ Approximately 8,000 teenage highway fatalities annually are alcohol related.[7]

▼ About one-half of all teenage homicides are associated with alcohol or other drugs.

And then there is the most frightening statistic of all:

▼ Children who are addicted to drugs and alcohol before age 18 have only a 50% change of living until they reach their 30th birthday.

Remember, Alcohol and Tobacco Are Drugs

In some ways, calling alcohol and tobacco gateway drugs may seem silly and outdated, a relic from the times when taking a drink or a smoke was a rite of passage performed only by a few. After all, if all kids use these drugs, then why should their use be more of a lure to other drugs than, say, the equally universal hamburgers and pizza?

There are three big reasons why the use of alcohol and tobacco, no matter how widespread or accepted, is different:

1. Drugs are a luxury. Food in some form is required by everyone, every day, but no one needs to abuse drugs to survive. If all drugs were to vanish tomorrow, the human race would still go on—and certainly be much the better for it. (Needed and vital prescription medications are sometimes found on lists of drugs: It is the overuse or abuse of these products that turns life-saving medicine into an unnecessary drug.)

---

[6] Lloyd D. Johnston, Patrick M. O'Malley and Jerald G. Bachman, *Drug Use, Drinking and Smoking: National Survey Results from High School, College and Young Adult Populations* (Rockville, MD, National Institute on Drug Abuse, 1989), 94, 100–103.

[7] Donald Ian Macdonald, "Patterns of Alcohol and Other Drug Use Among Adolescents," *Pediatric Clinics of North America* 34, no. 2 (April 1987): 276.

2. Drugs are addictive. It is not yet fully understood what makes an addictive personality. While it is certainly possible to be psychologically addicted to food or other ordinarily benign substances or to activities such as gambling, drugs have an added addictive potential. At the base of most drugs is a chemical that can take such a powerful hold on the body physically or psychologically or both, that only by an extraordinary effort can the person give it up. Alcoholics never become ex-alcoholics. They merely become alcoholics who do not drink.

3. Drugs are illicit. No matter the drug or its licit status in the world, the only purpose of taking a drug is to get high, and this is something your children know very well. Drugs' illicitness is part of their mystique, part of their attraction. Alcohol and other drug use signifies many things to children: a symbol of maturity, a connection with the adult world, an expression of rebellion, a sense of getting away with what is not approved.

Children know very well that they are not supposed to be using alcohol and tobacco, even if they may not understand where that use might lead. Even so, virtually all our kids eventually experiment with one or the other, and at ever earlier ages. Drugs are a universal.

Drugs: Running the Numbers

Twenty years ago, the sexual revolution supposedly destroyed the myth that there are "good" kids who don't and "bad" kids who do. Today, drugs are parents' worst nightmare, so awful that many parents absolutely refuse to believe that their children could ever be using them. These parents have a million ways to deny reality: Their children are different; they've been brought up right; they're exceptions. We hope so. All we have to go by are the statistics, and everyone knows that statistics on alcohol and other drug use, especially for children, are slippery things. When we offer you our statistics, we do so with the acknowledgment that we're pretty sure they're wrong. Only one thing . . . most likely, they're wrong on the *low* side.

The reason for this is the huge dropout rate in this country. "Drugs and Dropouts," a report based on hearings held before the Congressional Select Committee on Narcotics Abuse and Control in 1986, found that about 25% of all youth drop out before graduation from high school. The committee found that drugs and dropping out are associated with each other and that drug use is greater among dropouts. A separate study in Philadelphia stated that dropouts were almost twice as likely to be frequent drug users as high school graduates. But the number of studies in which researchers make the effort to track down and thoroughly interview dropouts about their drug use are few, so that the true extent of alcohol and other drug use among our children is hard to determine. So when reading any number that refers to drugs or drug use—including ours—take that number with a grain of salt.

Having said all that, there is one series of studies that are the model for everything else in the field. They aren't perfect (they don't really address the dropout problem, for example), but they do draw a more accurate picture of alcohol and other drug use of school-age children than anything else available.

Every year, researchers Lloyd D. Johnston, Patrick M. O'Malley and Jerald G. Bachman of the University of Michigan Institute for Social Research conduct a massive survey of high school seniors for the National Institute on Drug Abuse. (We will refer to it here as the Michigan Survey.) It's big: More than 16,000 students at about 130 high schools of all kinds, in every part of the country, answer questionnaires on their use of and attitudes toward drugs. Because the number of students is so large—10 times more than used by the Nielsen ratings—and so representative of the full spectrum of students, the answers given are held to have very high reliability. This is not only the largest continuing study but the oldest—having been done every year since 1975—so it gives us our best look at drug use today and how it has changed. The numbers are compelling.

From these surveys it is most likely that your children have tried drugs. The numbers change slightly from year to year, but an amazing 92% of high school seniors say they have tried alcohol at some point in their lives, notwithstanding the fact that the legal drinking age is now 21 in every state in the Union. About 67% of these students admit they have smoked tobacco. Perhaps most incredible is that 54% admit to having used an illicit drug—and this is actually the lowest percentage ever reported in the survey. The numbers are inescapable: With a small number of exceptions, by the time your children are out of school, they have tried a drug; certainly they spend much of their time around other children who have.

Why do so many children experiment with drugs? Perhaps it's because so few of them understand that just trying drugs—even the gateway drugs—can be harmful. About one-third of high school seniors think that taking four or five drinks nearly every day won't harm them. The percentages who think that trying small amounts of illicit drugs will be harmful are also alarmingly small: under 30% for amphetamines or barbiturates, under 20%

for marijuana, barely over half even for cocaine and heroin. A minimum of one high school senior in every 10 refuses to believe that he or she risks harm from the regular use of any drug. Kids who think that drugs are harmless will become kids who experiment with drugs.

The more students who try drugs, the more there are who are liable to keep on using them: occasionally, regularly or addictively. These are the active user, and though their percentage remains small, it is extremely significant, for here is the heart of the problem of abuse of alcohol and other drugs.

Among those who are active users, marijuana remains the illicit drug of choice: Nearly one-fifth of high school seniors used it within a month preceding the survey. Overall active use of other illicit drugs is quite small. No more than 5% of high school seniors admitted to using any other single illicit drug within the previous month. Two things must be kept in mind, however. One is that alcohol and other drug use varies widely from city to city and school to school. Cocaine, for example, is far more heavily used on the East and West coasts than in the South or Midwest. The second is that all figures on illicit drug use must be added to the massive amount of active use of alcohol. We now need to examine just how many of our children are in danger.

How Many Is Too Many: Current Drug Users

While percentages best put the entire drug picture in context, they are unsatisfying because they are so hard to visualize. In addition, in a huge country like the United States even a small percentage can translate into a monumental heartache for parents. If we ask how many alcohol and other drug users these percentages represent, it may be easier to understand why the entire alcohol and other drug care profession is being overwhelmed by the number of their clients.

The Michigan Survey asks seniors to say in which grade they first tried specific drugs. Based on these percentages we can work backward to provide an estimate of how many students at each grade level are at least experimenting with alcohol and other drugs. The numbers tell us that a total of 11 million students in grade six or above have tried alcohol and that close to 6 million have tried illicit drugs.

What about current users, those who have used drugs in the past month? Sixty-four percent of seniors drink—almost 2 million of them. No wonder that in contemporary teenage slang "to party" means simply to get drunk. Eighteen percent smoke marijuana—another 540,000. Hundreds of thousands of these youth actively use the incredible array of drugs, old and new, our children find all too easy to access: amphetamines and methamphet-amines, barbiturates, methaqualone, tranquilizers, methadone, heroin, morphine, codeine, opium, paregoric, nitrous oxide, amyl and butyl nitrate, solvents, Fentanyl, meperidine, hashish, mescaline, psilocybin, glue, LSD, DOM, STP, THC, DMT, PCP, MDMA (Ecstasy or Adam), Eve, Rhapsody and whatever may have happened to be invented and hit the street markets this morning.

Making the Nightmare Worse: Cocaine, aka Crack

And we left one drug off that incredible list. That drug is cocaine. Cocaine is not new, of course, either on the drug scene or in our schools. But it was never a major drug for children for one simple reason: It cost too much. Cocaine may have been the glamour drug of the stars, but only they could afford the thousands of dollars a week a full-blown cocaine habit could cost. Then in 1985 that all changed, suddenly and dramatically. A new form of smokable cocaine began appearing on big-city streets. On the East Coast it was known as crack, possibly for the crackling noise it makes while being processed; on the West Coast it received a descriptive name, rock.

By any name, crack is the strongest and most powerful type of cocaine now generally available. Not much is needed to get high, so it can be sold in minuscule and inexpensive quantities. A clear-plastic vial of crack costs not much more than a movie ticket or a cassette tape, something that just about any kid can afford. A crack high doesn't last very long, however—sometimes just a few minutes. Therefore, users need to come back over and over again, and addiction can follow more quickly than with any other drug.

Worse yet, crack can be deadly whether or not a person has reached the stage of addiction. Crack was implicated in the 1986 death of college basketball star Len Bias. Bias, obviously in impressive physical shape and not known to be a heavy cocaine user, died after a few hours of celebratory smoking with his friends.

The rewards of dealing crack are phenomenally high. An aggressive teenage dealer in New York City can make $3,000 a day. Nine- and ten-year-olds are recruited as lookouts to warn against police and are rewarded with as much as $100 a day. Schools are moving to ban gold jewelry, designer clothing, and beepers worn by drug dealers and those who are rushing to imitate what appears to be an alluring life-style. Ignored in the rush to glamour are the guns, beatings, torture, prostitution and drug-related killings.

United in a World of Drugs

While gang warfare with Uzi submachine guns is restricted to a few of the largest cities, the crack problem is not solely an inner-city concern. Much of the money to buy the drugs comes from the suburbs. Honor students are succumbing to crack as well as dropouts.[8] In fact, believing that any part of the drug problem is restricted to inner-city or minority youth is blinding yourself to the real world. Studies have clearly shown that white youth drink more and use drugs more often than either black or Hispanic youth.[9]

Every ethnic group uses drugs, though in wildly varying amounts. One study showed that about the same percentage of Asian girls drink as Asian boys, but while the girls virtually never wound up as heavy drinkers, the boys who drank averaged a staggering five drinks a day. Nearly one-third of Native American boys were heavy drinkers, and on average they used drugs almost twice as often as any other group. The aftermath of drug use also varied dramatically. Black girls drank almost as moderately as the Asian girls but racked up four times as many alcohol-related problems.[10]

One result appeared consistently: Groups that used more alcohol also used more of the other drugs.

No matter what your background, no matter where in the country you live, no matter what size city you live in, if your children are old enough to use drugs, you must be concerned about the possibility of their drug use.

---

8 Richard G. MacKenzie and Edward A. Jacobs, "Recognizing the Adolescent Drug Abuser," *Adolescent Medicine* 14, no. 1 (March 1987): 225–6.

9 John W. Welte and Grace M. Barnes, "Alcohol Use Among Adolescent Minority Groups," *Journal of Studies on Alcohol* 48, no. 4 (1987): 329–30.

10 Jerald G. Bachman et al., "Racial/Ethnic Differences in Smoking, Drinking, and Illicit Drug Use Among American High School Seniors, 1987–89," *American Journal of Public Health*, 81: no. 3 (March 1991): 375.

Parents: Shouldering Another Responsibility

Children are small bundles of curiosity. Whatever their age, they are consumed with the desire to know more about their world, to imitate their parents and try to act out the mysteries of adult life, to explore—by themselves and with their friends—all the sensations that come into reach. Drugs are a part of that world, one that can seem glitteringly enticing.

You can't shut off the curiosity of children, which means that there is every expectation that they will indeed try drugs and a good chance that they will try one or more of the illicit drugs.

As a parent, you may have noticed small changes in your child's behavior, changes that you may have told yourself could have any number of innocent explanations. Your child may be dropping out of sports or scouts or church groups and suddenly picking up an after-school job. Grades may be falling, with discipline problems on the upswing. You may notice small amounts of money disappearing. Your children may be suddenly moody and unpredictable.

For many kids these changes are simply components of the mysterious process of growing up. For others, illnesses, psychological problems or disturbances in the home or at school may be the cause. But as a parent you must be aware that a pattern of Red Flags may mean that your child has a problem with alcohol and other drugs. Your hope must be to recognize this and confront it—calmly and in control—at the earliest possible moment.

Confrontations with your children are never easy. As parents, though, you have responsibilities that cannot be denied. Being able to recognize the Red Flags of alcohol and other drug abuse is a critical skill for every parent in a time when drug use is rampant. We hope that this book will provide you with those skills and more—a good basic understanding of the reasons and realities of children's drug use and abuse and the ability to steer your children safely through the perilous world in which they live.

2

The Four Stages of Drug Abuse

Kids try drugs for a variety of reasons, none of which appear to them to be very dangerous, as we'll see in Chapter 4. Certainly, no kid experiments with alcohol or other drugs with the intent of becoming addicted. Even so, that first use of a drug puts them on a different path than those who never try drugs at all. To paraphrase the classic Chinese saying, this heartbreaking journey of a thousand miles begins with a single thoughtless step.

Those children who journey past experimentation toward abuse are not the innocents they were before. Kids on drugs drift away from friends and family; lose interest in school, sports and church; become angry, isolated and unreachable; and possibly even waste away physically. Few things can be harder for parents than seeing these changes without understanding why they are taking place. Drugs create a standard pattern of behaviors that are crucially important for you as parents to know.

Though we all like to think of ourselves and our children as unique, the truth is that the evolution of drug behavior is pretty much the same for everyone. By their very nature, many drugs are physically as well as psychologically addictive. Kids' behaviors toward drugs and drug use also follow set paths because they know that drug use is wrong and that they're committing crimes through buying drugs, owning drugs or stealing money to get more drugs.

This sets alcohol and other drug use aside from other activities kids have been known to overindulge in. As an example, kids may spend so many hours playing video games that friendships and schoolwork suffer. But someone can stop playing a video game with no harmful effects. After a certain point—a point that for some drugs, like crack, can come as early as the first use—that is no longer true for drugs. Drugs exert a physical pull on the body that—not for everyone, but for too many—only more drugs can satisfy. When this happens, behaviors are all too predictable.

To make it easier to understand these behaviors, let's separate them into four major stages. By understanding these stages, you will have all the information necessary to gauge the extent of your child's alcohol or other drug use. Understanding your child's behavior will allow you to make informed decisions about confronting your child's drug use.

Just Before That First Use

It's never too early to talk to your children about drugs. In today's world, in fact, you have to start early. If you wait until your children are in junior high, they may already have experimented with drugs. By the time they are only eight or nine, drugs are already so visible in their world that they can't be ignored. Remember, underlying much experimentation with drugs is simple curiosity.

If you're the kind of parent who can sit and talk with your kids, you may be able to satisfy their curiosity with an honest discussion about drugs and their effects. After all, kids do learn to look both ways before crossing a street. They learn not to touch hot stoves. An increasing number of children are learning not to try drugs at all.

When you talk with them, tell them that:

▼ Drugs are far more dangerous to someone their age than to adults.
▼ Physical addiction to certain drugs may take years in adults but can develop in weeks in children.
▼ Twenty-five percent of children who start smoking still have the habit 20 years later. And 85% to 95% of drug users are also cigarette smokers. If, however, they keep away from cigarettes while young, they'll probably never have a problem with smoking.
▼ Some people are more disposed to addiction than others, and there is no way to tell in advance which are which.
▼ The only guarantee of never acquiring the drug habit is never trying a drug.

Don't be surprised and discouraged if they don't listen. The odds are that you didn't listen when your parents tried to warn you about life's dangers. As we said in Chapter 1, the majority of kids will take that first step and experiment with a drug. Not doing so would cut that child off from an experience common to most children and most adults: a big price for the naturally curious to have to pay. That doesn't mean that it's right, only that parents must expect it to occur.

Stage 1: Learning the Mood Swing

When kids do try that first drug, they're going to go for one used by the people close to them—parents or friends. That means that their first drug is most likely to be tobacco or alcohol, although it is also possible that they might first try marijuana, inhalants (such as nail polish remover or plastic cement) or even crack. However, since refrigerators, liquor cabinets and table tops in the home are the easiest places for kids to find drugs, your kids' first drugs are probably going to be your own. All these beginner drugs are known as gateway drugs, because they open the gate to later, more persistent drug use.

Kids of all ages desperately want to be grown up. Much of their curiosity is driven by what the adults around them do. Imitating adult behavior starts with learning to say ma-ma and da-da and never lets up. Nobody has to go to school to learn how to talk or walk or how to get dressed or make a sandwich. Curiosity and learning work the same way with drugs. If you use drugs, so will your kids. Tim notes:

> When I talk to kids they always ask me the same question, "Why do adults preach to us not to use drugs and alcohol when my own mom or dad smokes a pack of cigarettes a day?" Kids know how bad cigarettes can be. They'll tell me, "On the side of the pack it says basically that cigarettes will kill you." I've had other kids tell me, "I see my dad drink a six-pack or two in front of the TV when the football game is on and then turn around and tell me not to get high or drink." The bottom line is that kids mimic what we do, not what we say.

Peer pressure is the other major reason why kids start drugs. One kid, older or simply more experienced, will offer a drug to another. For the inexperienced child, fear of being different, of not being accepted or of being thought chicken is usually stronger than fear of the drug or of what parents might say if they found out. If older brothers and sisters are wise in the way of drugs, their younger siblings will likely soon try drugs themselves. Tim got this frightening story from a fellow officer:

> There was a bright young 8-year-old who never got into trouble, had very good grades and was good in sports. His 14-year-old brother liked to smoke marijuana. The little brother went up to him and said he wanted to get high, "like you." "Wait until you're a man like me," big brother said, "then I'll show you how to get high."
>
> Little brother didn't want to wait. One day he snuck into his brother's room, found the marijuana and went with a friend to the basement because that's where big brother smoked. The two 8-year-olds got high on just one joint. Too high. Little brother told his friend, "I can stretch my neck six feet." "Go for it," said the friend. Our 8-year-old tied one end of a rope around a basement rafter and the other end around his neck, climbed up three steps of the basement stairs and jumped. His neck didn't stretch—it broke. Big brother summed it up. "I killed my brother," he said. He was right.

Notice that we still haven't said anything about wanting to get high. That motive is there, but it's minor. Go back into your own past. Recall your first experience with a drug, and remember that it probably wasn't all that pleasant. The stolen cigarette may have burned your mouth and caused a coughing jag; the beer or whiskey tasted horrible and may have sent you running to the toilet to throw up; that first puff of marijuana (for those who tried it) probably didn't get you stoned. If getting high were the sole end to drug use, hardly anyone would ever stay with it long enough to find out what being high means. At first, curiosity and the opportunity of an adult experience are far more important.

The problem is that this phase doesn't last long. You only have to look around you to know that millions of people do believe that getting high is a fun thing. Large numbers of children will persist in drug experimentation to the point in which getting high becomes a major factor in drug use. This is the dangerous point, because it leads the child into Stage 2 use.

Whether we're talking about drugs or video games or junk food, kids are into immediate gratification. For the Stage 1 user, the many pleasures of drugs far outweigh any fears about the consequences of heavy or long-term drug use. The fact that drugs are forbidden or illegal will only make them seem more fun. Those first cigarettes or drinks or puffs on a joint bring kids into an adult world, give them status with other youth, let them put one over on their parents and give them pleasure besides. Those are the lures of drugs. In Stage 1, getting high is only a small part of the game.

Unfortunately, there are few ways you can tell when children have entered Stage 1 unless you happen to catch them red-handed. You can try to check for the telltale smells of tobacco or marijuana or inhalants, or you might keep an eye out for your child returning drunk from a weekend party. Looking for these physical signs are your best bet: At this stage, behavioral changes are small and hard to detect. Most kids are clever enough to cover up occasional use without too much lying, and neither schoolwork nor home life is likely to be affected.

Since your children probably aren't going to worry much about occasional drug use, you have to do so for them. Too many parents are content to let such behavior continue and be relieved that it has gone no further. Worse, they may be relieved that their kids are using "just" alcohol and not the illicit drugs. This is a huge mistake. There is no such thing as responsible drug or alcohol use by youth. Even first-time experimentation with certain drugs can be debilitating or fatal. And, of course, the long-term use of gateway drugs such as alcohol and tobacco has very well publicized dangers.

And for a minority, perhaps one-third of all youth, the mood swings to euphoria become too pleasurable to resist. When parties are no fun without drugs or when drugs become a necessity to feel relaxed, your child has shifted over to Stage 2.

Stage 1 Summary

Most Common Drugs: Alcohol, tobacco, marijuana and inhalants.

Typical Use: At parties, under peer pressure, on weekends.
Substances, supplied by others, not bought.
Low tolerance makes it easy to get high.
Easy access in the home and from friends.

Behavior: No detectable changes.
Lying is moderate.

Feelings: Feels good with few consequences.

Stage 2: Feeling the Mood Swing

To teenagers, life is a series of extremes. Good times are purer fun than any adults may ever have again; problems seem more impossible and incapable of resolution. Grades, friends, acceptance, physical changes, family difficulties, dating and sex all produce enormous stress on a child. Everyday rejections become raging crises. If you've established good relations with your teens, they may come to you for advice and consolation. If not, youths sometimes turn to the one thing that offers relief, brings back the good times and makes the bad times a little more bearable: drugs.

In Stage 2, drug use moves beyond parties and enters everyday life. Good times, not curiosity, control behavior. If drugs are all that are making your kids feel good, then they're not going to be content with waiting for the weekend for the taste of a beer or cigarette. If they can't swipe their drugs from you at home, they'll find a steady supply someplace else. Buying drugs becomes a regular habit.

New drugs make their appearance in Stage 2. Your kid has already broken the taboo against drugs and gotten away with it. There's no reason now in his or her mind to stick to just one or two of the gateway drugs. Now, any of them may be tried. The effect isn't the same, though. Users develop tolerance to drugs and need more and stronger drugs to reach the same high. Whiskey, rum and vodka are drunk in addition to beer and wine. Hashish and hashish oil intensify marijuana's effects. To combat hangovers or to increase performance, amphetamines—uppers—are used by sleepy students or athletes striving to steady a shaky arm.

Using these potent drugs or even greater quantities of the gateway drugs exacts a price. In Stage 2, behavior begins to change, in ways noticeable and frightening to parents.

If your children are using drugs, their attitude toward school is often the first thing to change. Watch for a sudden drop in grades or indifference to schoolwork. Daytime drug use cuts heavily into a student's ability to concentrate and learn, and time spent high on weeknights takes away from time spent on homework. Drug side effects like hangovers and headaches also take their toll. Truancy may increase as the student cares less about school or needs the extra time to find a steady drug supply. Marijuana plays a double role here: Not only does it affect short-term memory and attention span, both crucial for learning, but its use is also associated with the loss of interest and desire that is known as "amotivational syndrome."

While the broad outlines of this stage are similar for most kids, the individual details vary from house to house. You know your kids best. Loss of motivation can show up in any number of ways. It's up to you to be on the alert for major changes in behavior. Look for your kids no longer caring about their favorite things. Be suspicious if they suddenly start describing schoolwork, after-school activities or church and family affairs as boring or uncool. Watch to see if their ambitions diminish or long-term goals recede. If kids lose their sense of accomplishment, rewarding activities will take a backseat to more drugs. Researchers aren't sure whether marijuana use causes this lack of motivation or simply reinforces it, and similar behaviors may also occur with the use of other drugs. In any case, it's a serious problem because these changes are likely to lead to others even less desirable.

Kids seek out others like themselves. Kids using drugs will seek out other drug users. Here we see a vicious cycle. The more kids hang around with truants and dropouts, the less likely they are to turn their own lives around. You may see your kids disappear into a shadowy world of friends you seldom see and seldom approve of. These "friends" won't come into your house. They may stay in the car when they come to pick up your child. Callers will hang up if a parent answers the phone.

In place of friends, your child has moved into a world of drug buddies. Drugs are the only thing keeping these kids together, so drugs—not sports, or games, or shopping—are what they do. Because of this, isolation and paranoia are characteristic traits for alcohol and other drug users who have advanced beyond Stage 1.

Even though most kids are natural actors, living a double life, pretending to be one person at home and another with friends, isn't easy. Keeping up their act will often cause stress, a type of stress that they'll find easiest to relieve by doing even more drugs. Some kids get a break though. Their parents don't believe that they're using drugs, no matter how obvious the use. This is called denial, and it's one of the biggest pitfalls for parents. We'll talk more about denial in Chapter 5.

Confronting a child who has been abusing drugs is hard and may provoke temper tantrums, lying and paranoia. Family life can shatter at this stage. You may have to work to get past your child's isolation. Kids on drugs may resist taking meals with their families or participating in family events. Parents may find them staying away for long hours or retreating to their room behind a barrage of loud music; strange dress or other symbols of rebellion are also characteristic of this stage. We provide some ideas for help in Chapter 12.

Intervention should begin at this stage. Rehabilitation is far easier at this stage than later. If drug use is not squarely confronted, drug highs may become all that is keeping the user going, and the child may progress to Stage 3.

Stage 2 Summary

Most Common Drugs:	Same as Stage 1, plus hash, hash oil and pills, mainly amphetamines (uppers) and barbiturates (downers).
Typical Use:	Planned use involves buying substances and later, solitary use. Tolerance may increase. Use is no longer restricted to weekends but occurs throughout the week. Use moves from choice to necessity.
Behavior:	Beginning of dual life. Changes in friends. Withdrawn and moody. Beginning of aggressive anger and "conning." Hobbies and extracurricular interests are given up.

School grades drop.
First blackouts, periods of inability to remember events, start to occur.
Use of slang starts to increase.
Beginning of verbal abuse.
Lying, borrowing and theft start.

Feelings: Pride in handling substance use.
Experiences euphoric highs.
Mild discomfort when coming down.

Stage 3: Preoccupation with the Mood Swing

In this stage, we see kids whose entire lives are built around getting drugs and getting high.

Here are the daily users, the ones who absolutely need drugs to get them through their waking hours. Few kids reach this stage, and most of the ones who do are older teens. Studies tell us that fewer than 5% of high school seniors use either alcohol or marijuana daily. The numbers for other drugs are even smaller. While the percentages are small, the abuses are large. In Stage 3, we find the kids who are the hard-core users, the ones who are working to destroy others in addition to themselves as they spread crime and misery in their quest for more and more drugs.

Getting and staying high is the Stage 3 user's daily goal. Drugs no longer give these users the same kick as before, so more drugs and more powerful drugs are needed. Those in Stage 3 start or intensify their use of cocaine, PCP, LSD and other more potent drugs, sometimes in combination because the kick is stronger that way. Dangers lurk everywhere here: Not only are larger doses of stronger drugs more dangerous to the body all by themselves, but the junk dealers add to boost the potency of the drugs can be even more deadly than the drugs themselves. Tim knows:

You have numerous drug dealers, so to attract more business he will "boost" or "lace" his drug with whatever he can get his hands on. For cocaine, rat poison is popular. Dealers also like to put speed in cocaine to give the drug

23

a "power punch" so the user experiences a big initial sensation. I've seen
one guy put similar stuff on powder cocaine and tell me "this is for the
dummies who knock on my door." He laughed and then said, "I tell them
I'm their buddy."

Just securing the amount of drugs they need becomes a problem for Stage 3 users. A drug habit can cost tens or hundreds of dollars a day. Where do these kids get that kind of money?

Well, many of them work for it. Sure, jobs offer kids the chance to learn useful skills, good habits—including dependability and punctuality—and the value of money. But don't assume that any kid who works must be a good kid, one not involved with drugs. Some kids work solely to feed their habits and will keep jobs long after they've destroyed themselves in school. Statistically, children who work are more likely to use drugs than those who do not. Why? They have the money.

There are other ways children buy drugs. Girls sometimes allow themselves to become the girlfriends of guys with a steady source of supply. From here it is a short step to prostitution. Boys aren't immune. Homosexual contacts may be made in the same way and for the same reasons.

Every cop knows that drug money is at the bottom of crime in one way or another. If you're the parents of a Stage 3 youth, you're going to find that money or valuables will regularly turn up missing from your home as your children take whatever they can to get drug money. If there's nothing at home to take, users will shoplift from stores or plan muggings or robberies. Most petty crime in the United States today is committed by drug users desperate for money for more drugs. In fact, 60% to 70% of all crime can be related to drug and alcohol use.

Some users figure out that the best way to keep a steady source of drugs for their habit is to sell them. And who do they sell them to? Most illicit drugs are sold to youth—and not by professionals but by their friends and schoolmates. Many of them will target younger kids as new sources of revenue. Drug dealers have a vested interest in getting other kids into drugs. As Tim says:

Drug dealers like to set up juveniles to do their dealing for them. They are aware
that juveniles will only get slapped on the wrist in most cases. The growing
number of gangs use this fact to full force. The juveniles take all the risks for
the dealer and insulate him. They like the big money that they're making even
though they get paid less for their risks than the adult dealers. This means more
money for the main supplier.

Obviously, behaviors like these are much harder to conceal from parents. You'll definitely see the consequences of Stage 3 use. Grades plummet, truancy becomes frequent and dropping out is highly probable. Sooner or later, the police come around to question illegal actions. Hanging around with drug dealers, pimps and thieves, users have little contact with old friends or positive influences. Lying becomes a necessity, then pathological. Anger, violence and pain are a constant part of their lives.

Not even the drugs will cover all the pain in Stage 3. Users may experience unexpected drug reactions such as flashbacks, when the hallucinations produced by drugs like LSD return long after the drug was taken. Overdoses—massive doses too much for the body to handle possibly inducing convulsions, coma or even death—may also take users unaware. Whereas Stage 1 and 2 users experience large swings from normality to euphoric highs from drugs, Stage 3 users find that any time spent away from drugs is actively painful. Downs become more severe; depression, a part of life. Cocaine especially can leave a depressed youth feeling worse after the high wears off than before the drug was used. In addition, cocaine abusers may experience a wide range of chronic health problems: rhinitis, headaches, palpitations, nausea and vomiting, sinus problems, poor appetite and weight loss. At odds with their familes and friends, ashamed of their stealing and dealing, children at this stage may consider suicide as an alternative. Thousands of youth kill themselves each year, and drugs are often a factor.

Unless they get out of the drug life, Stage 3 users have few choices. Getting them to admit their problems is very difficult, and forced intervention is costly and not always successful. As they slip further into drugs, Stage 4 is waiting.

Stage 3 Summary

Most Common Drugs:	Same as Stages 1 and 2, plus cocaine, PCP, LSD, mushrooms and opium.
Typical Use:	Cost increase due to high tolerance. Daily use. Solitary use increases. Always gets high. Attempts to cut down or stop use, but cannot. Overdoses and flashbacks first occur.

25

Behavior:	Behavior worsens.
	Non–drug-using friends are dropped.
	Open identification as a druggie.
	Lying becomes pathological.
	Stealing and dealing support increased costs.
	Failure at school, skipping school, droping out.
	Police incidents occur.
	Job loss.
	Verbal and physical fighting with family becomes chronic.
	Chronic cough starts.
	General health deteriorates.
Feelings:	Getting high controls person's life.
	Feels distressed when not high.
	Backswing into pain occurs due to guilt and shame.
	Progressive loss of self-worth.
	Illusions used to rationalize and suppress feelings.
	Suicidal thoughts start to surface.
	Being high is the user's perception of normal.

Stage 4: Doing Drugs to Feel Normal

Stage 4 use is almost beyond the scope of this book. By the time users get to Stage 4, they are seldom children any longer. Schools don't get to see them, since they've either grown too old or long since dropped out. Emergency room personnel, however, are very familiar with Stage 4 users. At this point, overdose, blackouts, amnesia, delirium tremens, malnutrition and a host of other ills surface.

Dependence on drugs is so heavy in Stage 4 that drugs are needed just to feel normal. The euphoric highs of earlier stages are rare except when huge and dangerous amounts of potent drugs are used. Users are constantly in financial trouble, but they can no longer hold down a steady job. They drift from place to place, partly because they no longer have homes and partly because they're known to the police as habitual criminals.

It's easy to find books that talk of the success stories—the Stage 4 users who clean up their act, get off drugs, and live productive lives. It happens, and you as parents can help make it happen, but the truth is that the success stories are rare. If this book has a purpose, it's to help you confront the problem long before Stage 4 is reached, at a point when you stand a much better chance of making a difference. Families with a Stage 4 user need to seek professional help.

If the user does agree to seek treatment, drop everything you're doing and get that person to a professional treatment center immediately. Stage 4 users can quickly change their mind about rehab: Their will power is very weak, and the strength of their drug habit can pull them back very easily. Support, total support by family and friends, is crucial when treatment starts, as we'll talk more about in Chapter 12.

Unless the user agrees to stop all drugs, there is only one other way off the road.

Stage 4 Summary

Most Common Drugs:	All drugs from earlier stages, plus heroin.
Typical Use:	Use is constant. Tolerance is very high, resulting in very high costs. No control over use. Cannot distinguish between being normal and being stoned. Overdoses occur frequently.
Behavior:	Total deterioration of physical health. Chronic cough. Frequent trouble with the police. Cannot keep jobs or continue activities. Volcanic anger. Aggression toward family and others. Severe paranoia. Blackouts. Flashbacks. Euphoric recall and repression are chronic.
Feelings:	Starts use at the depression pain point. Uses substances to function and feel normal. Guilt, remorse, shame and anxiety are chronic. Self-worth or ego is eroded to almost nothing. Suicidal thoughts are very frequent. Use is now compulsive.

3

Drugs and Drug Categories

Everybody agrees that cocaine, heroine and marijuana are drugs. Most people today understand that alcohol is a drug as well. Thousands of useful and sometimes life-preserving medications found in pharmacies are also called drugs. But the vast majority of people take these medications for quite different reasons than getting high. Only a small percentage abuse them for their mind-altering properties. These clear-cut, obvious examples of drugs may blind parents to the range of drugs that their children may be using.

Though few people think of them as such, the nicotine in tobacco and the caffeine in coffee are both extremely powerful drugs. Nicotine is now known to be one of the most physically addictive drugs, and misguided youngsters will sometimes pop caffeine pills in order to get high. Many other everyday household products, useful in a thousand ways, contain chemicals that can give a youth a quick and dangerous high. You could have these products in your kitchen for years and never think of them as drugs, but they are.

If your child is high on something that you never realized could be a drug, you're not likely to recognize the symptoms or the dangers of that drug. If you have never touched cocaine or PCP or LSD you are just as unlikely to be alert to their effects. Most people, in fact, couldn't identify the signs of drug use, unless the user is high on alcohol, whose effects are most commonly seen in our society.

As parents, it's important for you to have an idea of what individual drugs do. On the most basic level, it's easier to tell if your children are actually using drugs if you have an idea of what to look for. Identifying which stage (as detailed in Chapter 2) your child is in is easier if you know drug type, quantity and length of use as identifiers. Intervention can be aided if you can be specific about drugs your children are taking. You also need to know that some drugs are far more dangerous in the short term than others, more likely to produce harmful reactions or addiction. In the worst possible case—overdose—recognizing which type of drug was being used can literally be life saving.

Complete knowledge of drug effects is impossible. Hundreds of substances have been used as drugs, and some are very rare, or brand new; many produce different effects in small doses than in large ones. We've tried to simplify matters by dividing all drugs into a few basic categories following the classification scheme laid out in the Addiction Research Foundation's excellent and comprehensive guide *Drugs and Drug Abuse: A Reference Text* (second edition, revised 1987). Others group drugs in slightly different ways, but overall those distinctions are minor.

Drugs work on the chemistry of the body or the brain, either speeding up or slowing down physical processes or causing perceptual or behavioral changes that to parents and other outsiders will appear as bizarre behaviors. For example, all the speed-up drugs, known as stimulants, work in about the same way, with similar effects and common signs of use, so we'll discuss them all together. To make the listing even handier, we've set aside the most commonly used drugs in each category—marijuana, cocaine, LSD, among others—for specific treatment, since these are the ones you're by far the most likely to see. Looking for signs of drug use in others is not the same as feeling the effects of the drug on yourself, so we also have a special section on alcohol. Newer drugs that don't fall into the traditional categories—PCP and steroids, for example—also get special sections.

Each section has a common format:

Appearance
Included are both the form that a drug generally comes in—tablet, powder, liquid—and the way it is most often used—swallowed, snorted, smoked, injected.

Common Trade Names
Many drugs are abused prescription medications, often stolen from parents' medicine cabinets. For these drugs, we give the common trade names. These drugs also have chemical names, but children are less likely to call them by those names.

Street Names
You need to recognize street slang as readily as your children do so that you know when they are talking about drugs. We provide the most

common and widely used names, but be warned that new and localized terms pop up every day. Most drugs can also be referred to by their initials, for example: C—Cocaine, M—Morphine, R's—Ritalin, H—heroin. We don't list initials, but you should keep alert for them in addition to slang names.

Signs of Use
We provide a quick summary of the most obvious physical effects caused by the drug, effects that are visible with a close examination of a child's body.

Effects of Short-Term Use: Low to Moderate Dosage
These are roughly equivalent to the effects you would expect to see in Stage 1 and 2 users, kids who are beginning to experiment with a wide range of drugs and who have little tolerance for or interest in huge or often-repeated doses.

Effects of Short-Term Use: High Dosage
Roughly equivalent to late Stage 2 or Stage 3 use, in which greater quantities of a drug are needed to achieve the same effects.

Effects of Long-Term Use
Roughly equivalent to late Stage 3 or Stage 4 use, so that tolerances to the drug are high and debilitating physical effects from repeated drug use are also beginning to show.

Overdose
Although Stage 4 users are especially vulnerable, overdoses can happen at any stage, even from a first use. Drug overdoses should be treated by competent medical personnel only. Not only are the consequences of an overdose extremely severe, but those treating the patient also may be in danger when drugs like PCP are involved, as they may make the user violent.

Withdrawal Symptoms
Users do go off drugs, sometimes because they are genuinely trying to kick them, more often because their supply of or money for the drug has dried up. Some withdrawal symptoms can be mild, but children who are chronic abusers will suffer far worse effects. Children in withdrawal can be very sick and need close attention and care.

At this point we need to issue a few warnings:

1. There is no one telltale, give-away symptom that indicates the use of any particular drug. Drug effects not only copy one another from drug to drug

but also mimic many everyday ailments: nausea, runny noses, bloodshot eyes. *Always* look for a *pattern* of symptoms to indicate use.

2. The effects of any drug will vary greatly, depending on a child's individual characteristics (age, size, personality, tolerance) and the dosage of the drug. We will list a variety of effects—beginning with the more common—and it is highly unlikely that any one person would experience all of them.

3. Drugs are typically mixed with inert substances to add bulk and increase profit for the dealers. This lowers the drug's potency, which is bad for sales, so many dealers add small amounts of more powerful drugs—even poisons—to give their drugs an extra kick. These extras are even more likely to cause adverse reactions than the drugs themselves and can cause unpredictable reactions.

4. Children may use drugs from several different categories simultaneously, either for greater kicks or to mitigate the side effects of the drugs. Experienced users of one drug also may be beginning users of other drugs and will therefore show signs of two stages of use at once. Treatment centers are now discovering that the majority of their patients—80% or more—are cross-addicted, that is, using alcohol and one or several different other drugs.

5. New drugs are constantly introduced into the drug world. Most are variations on older drugs—crack cocaine, for example—or combinations of drugs already on the street—for instance, a heroin/crack mixture known as "crank" or "moon rocks." Occasionally a new "designer drug" will be synthesized with unpredictable results, or standard medications will suddenly start being abused by large numbers of youth, as happened with steroids. No book can be fully up to date with the street drug scene. Fortunately, the vast majority of new drugs or drug combinations fall squarely into the drug categories we present. And the progression of stages will be identical for all drugs. Even if you suspect that your children are using a new drug we do not specifically mention, the framework of knowledge and understanding that we lay out in this book will still apply.

Depressants

Virtually all the depressants are licit drugs, at least for adults. They are easily and readily available, can be bought and sold openly and, in one form or another, probably can be found in every household in the country. If you have reached adulthood in our society, it is overwhelmingly likely that you have already taken a depressant. But because they are so easy to come by, their potential for abuse is extremely high.

Alcohol is by far the best-known depressant and probably the most abused drug in the world. The most frequently prescribed and abused prescription medications are also depressants, including the barbiturates and nonbarbiturate tranquilizers such as Valium. And as if to ensure that there can be no escaping the depressants, dozens of everyday household products contain solvents or aerosols sniffable for euphoric—and very dangerous—highs with depressant effects.

Depressants get their name not because they cause people to become emotionally depressed—although that can be a result—but because in medical terms they cause a physical depression, or reduction, of the functions of the brain and other parts of the central nervous system. First to get reduced are the inhibitions that society has place on our brains. Without inhibitions we get the party behavior that makes people associate having a good time with drinking alcohol—and kids make this association as much as adults. The apparent stimulation that comes from a small dose of a depressant is what is technically called a paradoxical reaction. Unlike the true stimulants, higher doses of a sedative will cause sleepiness, stupor or even a coma.

At sufficiently high doses, depressants cause impairment to vision, perception and judgment, reduced coordination and an inability to divide attention, which results in concentration on one aspect of a task to the detriment of others. For all these reasons, driving, operating complex machinery or engaging in potentially dangerous behavior is doubly dangerous while under the influence of depressants.

Probably 90% of youth have tried alcohol by the time they finish high school. About 20% have experimented with inhalants and fewer than 10% have used barbiturates, sedatives or tranquilizers.

Alcohol

Hundreds of alcoholic beverages are in use throughout the world. Although selling them to minors is illegal in the United States, the evidence indicates that most youth in this country have easy access to alcohol. The alcohol content of different beverages varies widely, from about 0.5% for some types of reduced-alcohol beers to 75% for some rums. What matters, however, is the total amount of alcohol that a person drinks in the course of a drinking session—a bottle of beer, a glass of wine and a shot of liquor all contain about the same amount of alcohol.

Common Trade Names
Too many to mention.

Street Names
Booze, vino, brew.

Appearance
Cans, bottles, kegs and other containers.

Signs of Use
Smell on breath or clothes; slurred speech; red or glassy eyes; poor balance; cold and clammy skin.

Effects of Short-Term Use: Low to Moderate Dosage
Two patterns of behavior are common. One results in heightened activity, loud or unusual behavior, talkativeness and partying. The other may lead to drowsiness, withdrawal and hostility. Behavior is greatly affected by the amount used and the individual's level of tolerance. In either case, even moderately large doses will result in impaired judgment and memory, confusion, poor reflexes and slurred speech.

Effects of Short-Term Use: High Dosage
Exaggerated emotions and mood swings; inability to articulate; loss of motor control; blackouts; sleep; stupor; coma.

Effects of Long-Term Use
Depression; anxiety; blackouts; amnesia; socially unacceptable behavior; impotence; cirrhosis of the liver; cancer; brain damage; suicide (one in three suicides are alcohol related); violence.

Overdose
Stupor; cold and clammy skin; low body temperature; accelerated heart rate; coma; death.

Withdrawal Symptoms
Tremors; heavy sweating; weakness; agitation; headaches; nausea and vomiting; abdominal cramps; rapid heartbeat; hallucinations; seizures; delirium tremens.

Barbiturates, Tranquilizers and Nonbarbiturate Sedatives

The sedatives include some of the best-known and most widely prescribed prescription medications. Billions of these pills are manufactured every year. Some of these wind up directly on the street; many others are stolen from legitimate prescriptions held by parents.

Appearance
Pills or capsules of all shapes, sizes and colors.

Common Trade Names
Barbiturates: Seconal, Nembutal, Amytal, Luminal.
Tranquilizers: Xanax, Librium, Valium, Ativan, Serax.
Others: Placidyl, Doriden, Tualone, Noctec, Noludar. (Note: Quaalude and Sopor, once extremely popular, are no longer marketed in the United States.)

Street Names
Many names refer to the color of the individual pills: Blues or blue heavens (Amytal), yellow jackets (Nembutal), red birds or red devils (Seconal). Other names come from their effects: blockbusters, brain ticklers, courage pills, downers, sleepers, goofballs, tranks. One frightening name for these pills is candy.

Signs of Use
Mild to heavy sedation; mild euphoria; slurred speech; slow, unsteady gait; dizziness.

Effects of Short-Term Use: Low to Moderate Dosage
Tranquillity; relaxation; lethargy; mild memory loss; confusion; blurred or double vision; loss of motor control; nausea; constipation; dry mouth; hangover symptoms. Some people will show intoxicated behavior and euphoria; others, hostility, anxiety or depression.

Effects of Short-Term Use: High Dosage
Sedated appearance; intoxication; impaired motor functions; mood swings; short-term memory loss; hostile and erratic behavior.

Effects of Long-Term Use
Impaired thinking, memory and judgment; disorientation; confusion; slurred speech; muscle weakness; daytime anxiety; restlessness; depression; complaints of poor-quality sleep and inability to feel well rested.

Overdose

Slow, shallow and irregular breathing; constricted pupils followed by fixed dilated pupils; low body temperature; very low blood pressure; weak pulse; stupor; coma; death.

Withdrawal Symptoms

Nightmares; insomnia; panic reactions; tremors; depression; mood swings; hypersensitivity to light and sounds; irritability; loss of appetite and weight.

Inhalants

The solvents used in many everyday products can produce intoxication and euphoria very similar to that produced by other depressants. In addition, however, they can produce sensory distortions and hallucinogenic effects. There are hundreds of these solvents. They are found in cleaning fluids; nail polish remover; gasoline; glue; household, model and plastic cement; paint and lacquer thinner; lighter fluid; waxes; typewriter correcting fluid; general household cleaners; and many other products.

Fluorocarbon aerosols were once used for the same effect, although these are hard to come by now as they are largely being replaced due to fears of their role in reducing the ozone layer.

The drugs amyl nitrite and isobutyl nitrite are also widely used as inhalants, as are the medical anesthetics nitrous oxide, chloroform and ether where available.

Younger kids, with little money and limited access to other drugs, are especially attracted to the inhalants that can be found around the house. Their use is often easy to spot, as the odors of the chemicals will stick to the child's clothes, linger in the areas used and be found on the rags or bags used to sniff from.

Inhalants can be extremely dangerous because the solvents involved are known to cause heart, liver and kidney damage as well as brain and nerve damage. Deaths have been attributed to sniffing isobutyl nitrite, and students have been known to die from sniffing butane lighter fuel.

Appearance

Amyl nitrite is a yellowish liquid in small glass ampules that are broken so that the fumes can be inhaled. Butyl nitrite comes in small bottles. Nitrous oxide may be seen in a small, quarter-ounce metal cylinder or the pipe from an aerosol spray can. The solvents are poured into paper or plastic bags or onto handkerchiefs or rags and the fumes inhaled.

Common Trade Names
Too many to list.

Street Names
Glue, sniffer; locker room (isobutyl nitrite); laughing gas or whippits (nitrous oxide); poppers or snappers (amyl nitrite); rush, bolt, bullet, locker room or climax (butyl nitrite).

Signs of Use
Odors from solvents; sneezing and coughing; runny nose or nosebleeds; nausea; irritated eyes; slurred speech.

Effects of Short-Term Use
Drowsiness; euphoria; giddiness; numbness; fatigue; giddiness; talkativeness; lack of coordination and muscle weakness; loss of appetite; slowed reflexes; slurred speech; impaired judgment; sensitivity to light; increased heart beat; nasal inflammation and nosebleed; chest pains; joint pains; hangovers.

Effects of Long-Term Use
Muscle fatigue; difficulty in walking; weight loss; tremors; brain and nerve damage; liver and kidney damage.

Overdose
Sleep; stupor; asphyxiation (from sniffing from plastic bag over face); heart failure (SSD: Sudden Sniffing Death).

Withdrawal Symptoms
Usually mild: anxiety; depression; loss of appetite; irritability; nausea; tremors.

Stimulants

In their effects on the body, stimulants are the exact opposite of the depressants. By stimulating instead of depressing the central nervous system, senses are sharpened, not dulled: The body is woken up rather than put to sleep. In practice, however, there are many similarities between the two classes of drugs.

Like the depressants, most stimulants are legal drugs. They are, in fact, the most widely used drugs in the world if we include both caffeine and nicotine. Even more so than alcohol, these drugs are so common that in the past they were simply not considered to be drugs.

Nicotine is a particular problem for the young. Some 90% or more of smokers start as teenagers or even younger: Very, very few ever start smoking as adults. It is only recently that the long-term health problems caused by nicotine and other chemicals in tobacco have been understood as the major societal health hazards that they are. Hundreds of thousands of Americans die each year from smoking-related diseases.

The harmful effects of coffee are still being debated, and caffeine's role in them is also not determined. Use of pure caffeine in pill form is common among youths, however, and can be dangerous.

Whatever their long-term costs, the psychological addiction that hundreds of millions of people have to caffeine and nicotine means that, much like alcohol, they are considered an indispensable part of relaxation and enjoyment.

Many adults are also familiar with the effects of another class of stimulants, the amphetamines, long used by students, dieters and long-distance drivers to combat fatigue and to suppress appetites. Today, amphetamine drugs and their variants are being replaced by newer and less powerful stimulants, just as milder sedatives have replaced depressants like Valium and Quaaludes, which were widely misused.

Even though alcohol and nicotine really are much larger health problems, when people talk of the drug problem they are often referring to one other stimulant: cocaine or its variants, crack or rock. Cocaine stands out because it is an illicit drug and because of the sometimes devastating short-term harm it can bring. Cocaine is an extremely powerful stimulant and is especially dangerous to children. Whereas it takes an average of two to three years for adults to become addicted to powder cocaine, crack users can become addicted on their first try, and almost always will do so within three to six weeks.

Because the loss of inhibitions from low doses of depressants can produce euphoria similar to that caused by the stimulants, it can often be difficult for observers to distinguish between the effects of the two. (In fact, some nonamphetamine-type stimulant appetite suppressants will actually produce drowsiness and sedation.) Over the long haul, however, depressant users will slow down and tend toward sleep or stupor, while stimulant users will tend toward insomnia and activity.

Some stimulant use is universal and ordinarily harmless. Nearly every child receives caffeine from chocolate, cola beverages and tea. However, caffeine highs can be had more directly by taking commercially sold caffeine pills. Younger children are major users since, like inhalants, these are easy to obtain. Dealers, always looking to rip off their customers, sometimes sell caffeine pills in place of more expensive stimulants. About two-thirds of high-school seniors have smoked cigarettes, and about one in five has used amphetamines. Cocaine use is down under 15% and has been dropping for several years.

Cocaine

Cocaine in its basic form is a white powder and is usually sold that way on the street, always much diluted with other substances. Snorted into the nose, cocaine requires several minutes to produce a very intense high that needs continual boosting. Powder cocaine use among children is being phased out in favor of a variation called crack or rock. Crack can be 20 to 50 times purer than street cocaine and produces a high in just seconds. Because small quantities are needed, the street price is very low, although new hits are needed every 15 to 20 minutes. Freebasing is another way of purifying cocaine—by heating it with a solvent that removes the impurities—but the process requires expensive and dangerous chemicals. It is rarely used by youth.

Appearance
Cocaine is normally inhaled but sometimes smoked or added to cigarettes—either tobacco or marijuana. It can be injected, but this is rare. Crack comes in light brown pellets or small white chips or "rocks," often packaged in small vials. It can be smoked or heated in a spoon and its fumes inhaled.

Common Trade Names
None.

Street Names
Dozens exist, with more springing up all the time. Common ones are coke, snow, toot, flake, lady, white, nose candy, happy dust. Crack and rock are used interchangeably.

Signs of Use
Sniffles and/or runny nose; excitability; talkativeness; agitation; dilated pupils.

Effects of Short-Term Use: Low to Moderate Dosage
Euphoria; increased activity; loss of fatigue and appetite; increased heart rate and blood pressure; euphoria may be followed by agitation and anxiety.

Effects of Short-Term Use: High Dosage
Tremors; agitation; high blood pressure; headaches, pallor, weak pulse, nausea and vomiting; increased body temperature; cold sweats.

Effects of Long-Term Usage
Nervousness; agitation; excitability; mood swings; hallucinations; insomnia leading to exhaustion; appetite suppression alternating with intense hunger; impotence; high blood pressure; irregular heartbeat.

Overdose
Delirium; rapid, irregular, shallow respiration; convulsions; unconsciousness; death.

Withdrawal Symptoms
Exhaustion; depression; restless sleep with intense hunger on awakening; cravings for more.

Amphetamines

Amphetamines, like cocaine, can produce an intense rush, a feeling of well-being and excitement that is likened to an orgasm. One variation, the methamphetamines, is so potent that it is known as speed. Speed has a dark reputation because it can produce paranoia and violent behavior. The long history of abuse of amphetamines had led to the rise of non-amphetamine stimulants less potent and more tightly controlled. As a result amphetamine use has decreased significantly. Note: Long-term users will often use depressants to lessen the stimulant effect.

Appearance
Normally pills, tablets and capsules for swallowing. Methamphetamines show up as pills but also come in several variations—white powder, a paraffin-like block or crystalline form—that may be snorted or injected.

Common Trade Names
Amphetamines: Dexedrine; Desoxyn.
Others: Ritalin; Tenuate; Cylert; Didrex; Preludin.

Street Names
Amphetamines: uppers; pep pills; wake-ups; bennies; dexies; truck drivers; co-pilots; sky rockets; bombs.
Methamphetamines: meth; crystal; crank; speed.

Signs of Use
Intense feelings of strength and energy; hyperactivity; insomnia; loss of appetite; dilated pupils; increased heart and respiratory rate; elevated blood pressure; increased urine output.

Effects of Short-Term Use: Low to Moderate Dosage
Overstimulation; restlessness; dizziness; insomnia; euphoria; loss of appetite; increased energy and alertness; dry mouth; diarrhea.

Effects of Short-Term Use: High Dosage
Intense exhilaration and euphoria; increased physical strength; agitation; confusion; hallucinations; chest pain; fainting; excessive sweating; fever.

Effects of Long-Term Use
Chronic sleeping problems; anxiety and tension; loss of appetite to the point of nutritional deficiency; high blood pressure; rapid and irregular heartbeat; skin rash; paranoia.

Overdoses
High fever; convulsions; coma; cerebral hemorrhage; death.

Withdrawal Symptoms
Extreme fatigue followed by prolonged, disturbed sleep; voracious appetite on awakening; irritability; depression.

Hallucinogens

In some ways hallucinogens are the most druglike of drugs. Every other category of drugs has legitimate uses, even if they may wind up being abused. In contrast, the hallucinogens seem to have little purpose other than to twist the brain so that the everyday world turns bizarre. (Some components of marijuana, like THC, tetrahydrocannabinol, do have medical uses, such as controlling the nausea associated with chemotherapy.)

All the hallucinogens work directly on the brain rather than on the central nervous system. Although some physical effects are seen, hallucinogens are known for the vivid but distorted world they present to the senses, for their slowing of time and for the feeling that even the most trivial objects are important and profound. Despite their name, these drugs produce what are technically known as pseudohallucinations; users know that the effects they're experiencing aren't real.

One big problem with the hallucinogens is that their effects vary not only from person to person and by dose but also from use to use. Bad trips with all their resulting terror and paranoia may suddenly be experienced instead of the expected pleasant high.

Although some authorities place marijuana in a category of its own, we'll include it among the four main families of hallucinogens: marijuana and hashish; mescaline and MDA; LSD and psilocybin; and PCP.

Hallucinogens can be easily made by vendors who have some knowledge of chemistry, and an alphabet soup of designer drugs—TMA, STP, PMA, MMDA, and others—has emerged on the street. "Homemade acid" in a number of variations has also appeared, sometimes falsely claimed to be safer than 1960s LSD. More so than with other categories of drugs, users may get burned by substitutions. True mescaline and THC (the active ingredient in marijuana) are almost never found on the street, no matter what dealers may offer.

This substitution of one drug for another gets especially dangerous when PCP is involved. PCP, also known as angel dust, has so many different effects that it's almost a category unto itself. Most of these effects are damaging, and bad trips are all but a certainty. Despite this, the drug is so potent that dealers will often lace other drugs with it to boost their impact.

The hallucinogens are not considered to be physically addicting. Except for PCP, overdoses are unknown and withdrawal symptoms unlikely.

Marijuana is by far the most commonly used of the hallucinogens. Half of all high school seniors have tried it at some point. Despite their publicity, the other hallucinogens are relatively rare. Only about 1 in 10 students has ever used any. Although drug mixing makes it hard to know for sure, reported PCP use is lower than that for any other drug except heroin.

Marijuana

Marijuana and hashish are different versions of the same drug—they're made from the same plant. Marijuana is far more powerful today than in its heyday in the 1960s because it now comes with a higher percentage of its active component, THC (tetrahydrocannabinol). Hashish and hashish oil have even higher concentrations. In everyday use, marijuana may produce symptoms closer to those of alcohol than those of the other hallucinogens. Several long-term health risks from regular use of marijuana are suspected, including lung cancer from the high concentration of tar in a single joint, equivalent to 10 to 20 cigarettes. As with tobacco, these health problems are unlikely to be seen in youth.

Appearance
Marijuana is a mixture of small leaves with, usually, stems and seeds; it resembles parsley or oregano. It is almost always smoked in hand-rolled cigarettes or in pipes. Hashish comes in brown or black balls or bricks. Hashish oil is a syrupy liquid, often used to enhance a cigarette or marijuana joint.

Common Trade Names
None.

Street Names
Pot and grass are terms so commonly used that virtually everyone in America knows that they mean marijuana. Other typical names are bhang, dope, ganja, hemp and weed. Sinse (from sinsemilla) means seedless marijuana. Joints, jays, sticks and doobies refer to marijuana cigarettes. Reefer, for marijuana cigarette, is a very old term that was once virtually obsolete, although there are indications it may be making a comeback. Hashish is always known simply as hash. Although most marijuana is grown domestically (it is estimated to be the nation's largest cash crop), foreign varieties have better reputations and are often named according to their place of origin: Acapulco Gold, Panama Red, Maui Wowie, Mauna Loa, Mexican. Marijuana treated with PCP is called supergrass, crystal joints or killer weed.

Signs of Use
Sweet smell on breath, hair or clothes; giggling; euphoria; bloodshot eyes; coughing; increased appetite (the munchies).

Short-Term Use: Low to Moderate Dosage
Release of inhibitions; talkativeness or occasional withdrawn silence; relaxation; drowsiness; sense of well-being; impaired driving ability; increased heart beat; dry mouth and throat.

Short-Term Use: High Dosage
Hallucinations; impaired judgment and reaction time; confusion of time sense; paranoia; agitation; panicky feelings.

Long-Term Use
"Amotivational syndrome": diminished drive, lessened ambition, apathy, shortened attention span; poor judgment; impaired communication skills; impaired memory and concentration; bronchitis; asthma; sore throat.

Overdose
None.

Withdrawal Symptoms
Symptoms are usually mild: sleep disturbances; loss of appetite; irritability; nervousness; anxiety; sweating; upset stomach.

LSD, Psilocybin, Mescaline and Designer Drugs
Like marijuana, the peyote cactus is a plant whose parts are psychoactive, that is, have the mind-expanding properties users crave. Mescaline can be derived from peyote or produced synthetically. Psilocybin is also organic in origin and is derived from the Psilocybe mushroom, commonly found in Mexico and Central America. However, when people talk about hallucinogens, they usually mean a variety of synthetic drugs, especially LSD (lysergic acid diethylamide) or any number of synthetic street drugs. These latter, sometimes called designer drugs, include DMT (dimethyltryptamine); MDA (3,4-methylenedioxyamphetamine); STP, also known as DOM (2,5-dimethoxy-4-methylamphetamine); TMA and PMA (tri- and para-methoxyamphetamine); and MMDA (3-methoxy-4,5-MDA). As indicated by the amphetamines in their names, these drugs are related to the stimulants and may cause euphoric behavior in addition to hallucinations. LSD may cause the nervous system to lose control over muscles, leaving the victim unable to move, a condition known as freezing or jamming.

Appearance
A dose of LSD is far too small to see. What is sold are pills, sugar cubes or blotter paper impregnated with an LSD solution. These are then ingested. Mescal buttons are the brown, dried crowns of the peyote cactus. The buttons are chewed or ground up and smoked with tobacco. Mescaline is the refined form and comes in powders, capsules or liquid so it can be snorted, eaten or injected. Psilocybin was originally derived from an edible mushroom but can also be produced synthetically in forms similar to

mescaline. The designer drugs come in snortable powder form or in tablets or capsules.

Common Trade Names
None.

Street Names
LSD is universally known as acid but also has hundreds of local descriptive names, depending on appearance: sugar cubes, blotter acid, brown dots, blue heaven, orange sunshine and a rainbow of others. Mescaline and peyote are called mesc, cactus or buttons. Psilocybin is called sacred or magic mushrooms. STP supposedly got its initials from its names: serenity, tranquility, peace. DMT is known as the businessman's special.

Signs of Use
Distortion of reality; dilated pupils; dry mouth, sweating; if bad trip: paranoia; anxiety; panic.

Short-Term Use (symptoms do not change with larger doses)
Increased heart rate; rise in blood pressure and body temperature; tremors; increased salivation; nausea.

Long-Term Use
Bad trips; flashbacks; freezing and jamming (loss of control over muscles).

Overdoses
None.

Withdrawal Symptoms
None.

PCP (Phencyclidine)

PCP is a strange drug. Many authorities place it in a category of its own because it can mimic effects from all the other drug categories simultaneously. At low doses it can act as a stimulant, increasing heart rate and blood pressure, and at the same time work as depressants do, destroying muscular coordination and slowing respiration. These effects intensify at higher dosages. Emergency room personnel know that users can be nearly comatose one minute and violent the next. Users gain such strength and immunity to pain that they have been known to break police handcuffs. If they injure themselves, they may not even realize it until the effects of the drug have worn off. PCP is entirely unpredictable; its effects will change from user to user and from use to use. It produces extremely quick reactions when smoked. For this reason it is often substituted for or added to other drugs for a quick high that can be very dangerous to the unsuspecting user.

Appearance
Granular crystals to be sprinkled on tobacco or marijuana and smoked. A fine powdered form is snorted. It can also be found as a pill or in liquid form to be injected.

Common Trade Names
None.

Street Names
Angel dust; hog; pig, horse or elephant tranquilizer. When mixed with marijuana: superweed; killer weed; crystal joints.

Signs of Use
Blurred vision; constricted pupils; slurred speech; sweating; cramps; nausea.

Short-Term Use: Low to Moderate Dosage
Pleasant: euphoria; relaxation or stimulation; weightlessness; floating; time and space distortion.
Unpleasant: anxiety; agitation; paranoia; panic; terror; confusion; blank stares; stupor; rigidity; inability to speak; alienation; depression.
Physical effects are the same in either case: increased blood pressure and heart rate; shallow, rapid breathing; increased urine output; sweating; nausea and vomiting.

Short-Term Use: High Dosage
Intensification of unpleasant effects: erratic and bizarre behavior; incoherent speech; disorientation; paranoia; violent behavior; panic; terror; fear of death; alternating abnormally high and low blood pressure; slow, shallow and irregular breathing; severe nausea and vomiting; heavy salivation; decreased urine output.

Long-Term Use
Impairment of thinking and memory; flashbacks; speech problems (stuttering, slurred speech or inability to talk at all); severe anxiety and depression; paranoia; violence; suicide.

Overdose
Coma; convulsions; death.

Withdrawal Symptoms
None.

Narcotics

Throughout their history, humans have sought ways of killing the pain from wounds, accidents and disease. This is what narcotics do: Their very name means to numb or deaden. Physicians leaped on each narcotic as it was invented, touting it as the latest wonder drug, only to find that the cure was sometimes worse than the disease.

Opium came first, then morphine and codeine were refined from opium, and later heroin and other drugs were developed from those. These naturally occurring narcotics are known as the opiates. Synthetic forms, not refined from opium, have been developed in recent years to produce the beneficial pain-killing effects of the opiates without the physical dependence they bring. Despite the once-common image of the heroin user as the ultimate drug abuser, heroin use among youth is relatively rare, with only about one user in a hundred. Abuse of the synthetic prescription drugs is far more common, but collectively narcotics are the least-used drugs, with only 10% of high school seniors ever having tried them.

New users, who haven't worked up a tolerance to these drugs, may soon stop trying them because their first uses are likely to be extremely unpleasant. Nausea and vomiting are common side effects. In time these symptoms go away, but they're bad enough to discourage many users before they can get to the point of enjoying the experience.

The effects of narcotics are somewhat more predictable than those of the other categories of drugs, with all forms leading generally to euphoria at low doses and a zonked-out numbness at high doses. Constipation is almost always a side effect. While it is a myth that a single use leads to addiction, the narcotics are indeed heavily addicting. Heavy users go through severe and prolonged withdrawal if their supplies are cut off. Overdoses are also common, although death from overdose is probably rare. The synthetic narcotics are generally less dangerous than are the opiates.

Appearance
Heroin: white or brown powder; smoked, snorted or injected.

Morphine: white crystals, tablets or liquid; smoked, taken orally or injected.

Codeine: by itself, a dark brown liquid; often as part of a prescription cough medicine or pain pill.

Opium: dark brown chunks or powder; smoked or injected.

Dilaudid, Darvon, Demerol, Percodan, Talwin: pills, capsules, or tablets.

Common Trade Names

Meperidine—Demerol; hydromorphone—Dilaudid; oxycodone—Percodan; pentazocine—Talwin; propoxyphene—Darvon; methadone—Dolophine.

Street Names

Heroin: horse, smack, brown sugar, China white, junk, stuff and shit.

Morphine: Miss Emma, unkie, morph.

Codeine: schoolboy.

Dilaudid: doctors, lords.

Opium: dreamer, poppy.

Methadone: meth, dollies, methadose.

Signs of Use

Constricted pupils; head nodding; watery eyes; droopy eyelids; fresh injection marks; itching or burning skin.

Effects of Short-Term Use: Low to Moderate Dosage

Euphoria; sense of well-being; relaxation and drowsiness *or* talkativeness and activity; lightheadedness; dizziness; weakness; drowsiness; inability to concentrate; apathy; increased urine output; nausea and vomiting; sweating; decreased response to pain.

Effects of Short-Term Use: High Dosage

Intensification of low-dose symptoms plus sleep; slow, shallow breathing; decreased blood pressure; slower heart rate.

Effects of Long-Term Use

Physical and psychological deterioration; mood swings; constipation; scarring and collapsed veins from injections.

Overdose

Pinpoint pupils; cold and clammy skin; low blood pressure; slow and irregular heart rate; low body temperature; deep sleep; stupor; coma; death.

Withdrawal Symptoms

Yawning; agitation; tremors; depression; loss of appetite; dilated pupils; chills alternating with flushing; excessive sweating; watery eyes; runny nose; nausea; vomiting; abdominal cramps; muscle pain and spasms; pain in bones.

Steroids

At the onset of puberty, boys start producing quantities of the steroid hormone testosterone, causing them to go through a series of anabolic changes, those concerned with growth and the development of muscle and body tissue. They also go through another set of changes known as androgenic, the ones responsible for hair growth, deepening of the voice and development of sex organs. Pharmaceutical manufacturers have worked for many years to synthesize drugs that would cause the body to mimic the desired anabolic effects without also undergoing the androgenic ones. None have completely succeeded. Still, the demand for these drugs, commonly known as anabolic steroids, is so great that a flood of steroid medications has entered the market.

Anabolic growth is exactly what athletes in most sports and at all levels are looking for. Steroids that promote this effect provide a rapid way of putting on the extra weight and muscle that seem to be necessary for success. Bodybuilders, weight lifters, field athletes and football players are the main users, especially since steroid use also increases aggression—a trait that, rightly or wrongly, is rewarded in the playing field, but may lead to numerous problems elsewhere.

The extent to which anabolic steroids have infiltrated professional and amateur sports is not known, although athletes who have relied on the drugs routinely place the percentage of users very high. Steroid use is seldom admitted publicly, and new revelations about this use, from athletes who have vehemently denied taking the drugs, have had the unfortunate effect of leaving all athletes suspect. Though at one time doctors denied that steroid use improved performance, events have forced them to admit they were wrong. Olympic gold medal sprinter Ben Johnson has not been able to come anywhere near his world-record time in the 1988 Olympics since freeing himself from a steroid regimen. Others, particularly football players, have attributed their making the professional ranks to the enormous masses of muscles that steroid use made possible.

Despite the recent stories and articles about the consequences of steroid use, the drugs have infiltrated our schools. One study has estimated that

500,000 high school seniors have tried anabolic steroids, which would make its use as common as cocaine, and there is convincing evidence that it is also being used by younger children. An alarming trend is the use of steroids among nonathletes, just to improve appearance. Some 15% to 20% of high school users are thought to be nonathletes.

There are two major classes of steroids: tablets, which may be swallowed or dissolved under the tongue; and liquids to be injected. Some users prefer the oral tablets because their use does not leave visible needle marks. However, oral anabolic steroids are more toxic, increase liver damage and must be taken every day since they are processed in the body within 24 hours. Injectable steroids are more common since they do not need to be taken as often; they can stay in the body for as long as a month, depending on the rate at which the drug is metabolized. Users also run the risk of an allergic reaction to the drug, especially if the drug is procured on the street and is contaminated. As a general rule, the greater the androgenic effects of the drug, the more dangerous it is to the hormone system and the liver.

Steroids are taken for a set amount of time, usually six to ten weeks, following which users are supposed to let their bodies rest an equivalent period of time. This period of use and nonuse is known as a steroid cycle. Cycles have gotten longer at the same time that dosages have increased, with many users taking 10 times the recommended dosage or more. Athletes have also been known to keep injecting the drug right through the period they were supposed to let their bodies rest, thereby increasing the strain on them. Worse, many athletes "stack" or use several drugs simultaneously to try to minimize side effects or produce effects faster, only to increase the long-term damage they are doing.

In 1990, the legal status of anabolic steroids changed with the passage of the Anabolic Steroid Control Act. This law characterized steroids as controlled substances, making them illegal to possess, prescribe or distribute except for legitimate medical reasons. Heavy penalties have been attached to the law so that law enforcement officials can go after those who are dealing the drugs on the black market. Under the law, steroids have been classified as Schedule III drugs. Schedule III drugs are defined as those that have currently accepted medical uses but whose use may lead to moderate or low physical dependence or high psychological dependence.

Although a few dedicated people can achieve the masses of muscle required for entrance into the top ranks of such sports as football, wrestling and bodybuilding solely by working out, most need artificial help. Total muscle growth of 80 to 100 pounds has been known. With your child, watch for extreme and sudden body growth—up to 20 pounds of muscle in six weeks. One or two such cycles of steroid use should produce the symptoms listed under short-term use. Continued use over years or even several sports seasons may be sufficient to produce the long-term effects listed. Today, needle tracks are more likely to indicate steroid use than heroin or other drug use. At least one confirmed case of AIDS is known from sharing contaminated needles. Fortunately, many of the side effects of steroids will reverse or disappear when steroid use ends, although psychological effects such as depression, lethargy and inadequacy may be noticed during the immediate withdrawal period.

Appearance
Tablets, capsules, injectable vials.

Common Trade Names
Oral: Anadrol; Anavar; Dianabol; Maxibolin; Winstrol.
Injectable: Deca-durabolin; Depo-testosterone; Durabolin; Parabolin; Primabolan-depot.

Street Names
Roids, juice.

Signs of Use
Sudden growth in muscle mass; severe acne; pink and puffy skin; swollen face and neck; very tight skin over muscles; pronounced stretch marks; hair loss; jaundice; purple or red spots on body; bruising, even with slight injuries; swelling of feet and lower legs; trembling; unexplained darkening of the skin; persistent unpleasant breath odor; sudden hair growth or loss; violent, aggressive behavior.

Effects of Short-Term Use
Muscle and weight gain; fluid retention; high blood pressure; increased heartbeat; disturbed sleep patterns; breast enlargement; growth of body hair.
In girls: disrupted menstrual cycles; increased facial hair; permanent deepening of the voice.

Effects of Long-Term Use
Lowered sex drive; shrinking of testicles; liver disease; depression; insomnia; hyperactivity; violent behavior (roid rage); coronary heart disease; chromosome damage; stunted growth if used before puberty.

Overdose
None.

Withdrawal Symptoms
Loss of muscle mass; increased body fat; lowered energy and sex drive; severe depression; feelings of weakness as body size decreases; lethargy and listlessness; lack of interest in exercise or sports.

4

Reasons Why Kids Use Drugs

In Chapter 2 we outlined stages of drug use, from the first experimentation with drugs, through drugs as a part of everyday life, to drugs used as an end in themselves. Most kids try drugs, but few wind up submerging their lives in them: No magic answers exist to help parents understand which of their children will go on to this self-destructive behavior and why. Whatever situation your kids are in, your understanding of why your children are using drugs will provide important clues for intervention and treatment later on.

In this chapter, we sort the major reasons for drug experimentation and continued use, discussing these reasons in relation to the stages to which they most directly correspond. Please note that these reasons are presented in a special order. With the later reasons, it is more likely that the user will wind up in Stage 3 or 4. Progression into these later stages is therefore more likely the deeper we get into this chapter. You'll find that the first reasons are the most common ones, as most children never go past Stage 1 or 2. Later reasons will not be as obvious, since much heavy drug use is a denial of or escape from serious problems in one's life.

1. **To get high.** Taking drugs and alcohol simply to get high, for the good feelings they bring, seems so obvious that it is often overlooked by people who feel compelled to come up with a deep-seated reason for all behavior. All the same, wanting to feel good is a basic human motive. While it may be true that no one *needs* drugs or alcohol to have a good time, if you examine your own life-style you'll probably find that you consider some drug—probably alcohol, tobacco or coffee—a requirement. You may not overindulge; you may be quite moderate in your use. You tell yourself that you can handle it. If so, you are a part of the vast

majority of adults who are Stage 1 and 2 users.

Kids' reasons for using drugs are the same as adults. And they use drugs, especially alcohol, where and when and how adults indulge—at parties, at sporting events, as a reward, with friends. Slang terms of the youth culture—feeling good, partying, tanking up, being stoned, buzzed or wasted—attest to the most common urge among drug-using youth: getting high, usually as part of a crowd.

Drugs do make people feel good: That's why they've remained so popular for many thousands of years. Just the same, there are other, more valid and safer ways of securing pleasure. Heavy drug use actually negates the pleasures users get from small doses. For this reason, most kids who do drugs to get high never go beyond Stage 1 or 2.

2. **Curiosity and boredom.** Curiosity and boredom are flip sides of the same coin. Both send kids out looking for adventure and excitement, for new experiences, acquaintances, skills and abilities, for a chance to fill empty time and have more fun than school, work, chores or something they've been told to do. Drugs are a tempting answer to their search.

Curiosity is the natural state of youth. Think about how many times you've had to say "No!" to your children or needed to rush over and rescue them from a window ledge or electric plug. Despite the dangers it can lead to, curiosity is a requirement for kids. Without it they would never learn to walk, to read and write, to understand how the world around them functions. Anything new and different is an attraction for youth, especially if it is also a part of the seductive and fascinating adult world.

Drugs supply endless opportunities for satisfying this curiosity. In fact, curiosity is probably a far more important reason for enticing children into Stage 1 than is getting high. Though it may be hard to believe, a lot of kids are disappointed by drugs. They don't like the taste in their mouth after smoking a cigarette, the headaches that come from inhalants, the hangover from an alcohol binge. A lot of them stop at this point and never get any further.

Others remain curious about the good effects they keep hearing that drugs are supposed to have, and so they never stop. They keep trying more drugs or different drugs or new combinations of drugs until they explore all their possible effects. And because there are so many drugs, there is always another drug to try, always some new way to try it. Curiosity takes them past the gateway drugs and into more exotic substances—pills, LSD, cocaine, PCP, heroin. Though only a small percentage of youth go down this path, curiosity can lead users into Stage

53

3 before they are aware of it. From there the drugs take over.

Much of what we just said applies to boredom as well. Every parent knows how easily kids who seem to have every conceivable toy, loads of friends and active imaginations can still get bored. Boredom will entice kids into trying things they know they shouldn't be doing. Drugs are about the greatest time wasters ever invented. Seeking them out can waste away an afternoon and be an adventure at the same time, if stealing alcohol from home or trying to buy beer with a fake I.D. or searching out a local pusher is involved. The rituals of drug use take up more time: rolling joints, loading pipes, working through a six-pack. In addition, the drugs themselves both distort the time sense and fill the passing of empty time with a glow.

Kids live in the here and now. They don't put off good times the way adults can. They live for immediate gratification, which is one of the reasons they get bored so easily. Drugs satisfy this need as well. Drugs work right away and remain working as long as they are taken.

Kids who are particularly prone to boredom may have other problems: learning disabilities that prevent them from spending time with books or social or behavioral difficulties that keep them apart from other youth. Many other kids are growing up in worlds without video games, concerned parents or convenient recreational facilities. When the future looks as boring and hopeless as the present, drugs may seem to be an attractive answer. The harder the root problem is to solve, the more likely it is to lead to Stage 3 or 4 use.

3. Peer-group influence. If you want to know whether your kids are using drugs, ask if their best friends are. If the answer is yes, you have a problem.

Parents all know the line "but everybody else is doing it." Usually parents can show up the silliness of such an excuse with one favorite cliche, "If everybody else jumped off a bridge, would you do it too?" But here parents run into a huge problem: When it comes to drugs, the answer is yes, kids will jump off that bridge as long as it means they jump with their friends.

Kids don't think about peer pressure; they just want to be accepted. Being different is about the cruelest fate a kid can conceive of. If trying a beer or smoking a joint is required to be one of the gang, that seems like a small price to pay. It works the other way around as well: A kid who is the only one using drugs will try to pass the habit along to others to keep from being alone.

Thus, peer pressure is one of the major reasons kids try drugs in the first place and so enter Stage 1. It's equally important in forcing kids to stay users and so enter Stage 2.

The pressure to do drugs may come from anyone. Group pressure can be particularly intense. When drugs infect some members of a sports team, scout group, club, fraternity or any group in which team spirit or group solidarity comes into play, the pressure on the rest to join in will be massive. (Peer pressure has played a major part in the spread of steroid use among athletes at all levels. If not using steroids makes someone less of a player, that person no longer is as useful to the team.)

Groups provide an ideal environment for spreading drug use. They give kids an excuse to go off by themselves, make experimenting with and sharing drugs easy, allow one expert to teach skills and make it very hard for any individual to resist the others and still remain a part of that group.

When "partying" has come to mean "drinking" in teen slang, you know what is going on at those parties. Studies have shown that most teen drinking does indeed take place at parties, with only a comparatively small fraction of teens drinking steadily the rest of the week. Weekend binges result in as many as one-third of high school seniors getting drunk at least every other Saturday night. Parties in which heavy drinking takes place are probably unsupervised parties, an ideal environment for other drug use to occur as well. Such parties are bound to be favorites of teen groups. When this kind of behavior is the norm, abstinence cuts kids off from their whole social scene.

But individuals can also create enormous pressure. Few younger brothers or sisters could resist if their older siblings offered to share drugs with them. Since Stage 3 users may also be selling drugs to feed their habit, they may get their family involved as an efficient way of increasing their business. Guys also use alcohol and drugs as a means of breaking down their girlfriends' sexual resistance and inhibitions. Drugs have played a large and unacknowledged role in fueling the sexual explosion among teens and younger kids.

Kids who don't fit in anywhere else have found that by using drugs they will be treated as an equal in the largest club in the country: the club of drugs. No special skills or abilities are required, and even money is usually not too much of a problem at first. Drugs are a great leveler; they'll cut all kids down to the same size.

Adolescent rebellion is also a factor in drug use. Kids want to do what gets the approval of other kids, especially if it drives their parents wild. Loud music, strange clothing and stranger haircuts have proved successful at this since the 1950s. In the 1960s, kids discovered that doing drugs as a rejection of their parents' values would have even more of an effect.

The youth culture of the 1960s is long gone, but to this day drugs probably do more to upset more parents than anything else kids can try. Don't misunderstand. We're not saying that kids take drugs for no other reason than to bug their parents; rather, that drugs are part of a larger strategy of rebellion and solidarity with peers that creates many of the battles during the teen years and makes it much harder for anything parents can say against drugs to have any effect.

Whatever the pressures of conformity that drive youth in to using drugs, the danger is that drug taking can get out of hand. Kids often spend more hours with their peers than with their parents. If drugs are what their friends do, they'll follow along. Stopping may be next to impossible without abandoning the group, absolutely the last thing the child wants.

Drugs drive their users together. After a time, all of a kid's friends may be drug users, with drugs the only glue keeping the group solid. In this situation, Stage 3 or even Stage 4 use is sure to follow. Even for kids who maintain their social links to groups outside their drug world, continued drug use has its dangers. What starts out as a lark between friends can end up in troubles beyond what they could ever imagine.

4. Escape from outside problems. Many of the problems kids face are age-old. School has always been a hassle, parents' expectations high, sex a tantalizing but frustrating mystery. Poverty and prejudice have curtailed opportunities for countless youth who could have made more of their lives. Adolescence has never been easy.

None of these problems has disappeared, but a host of new ones now add stresses that increase the pressures on nearly every child. The highest rate of divorce in our history plus huge numbers of babies born out of wedlock have created more single-parent households than ever before. Most parents, whether in one- or two-parent households, are working outside the home, raising a generation of latchkey kids. Job transfers or the lure of better jobs in other communities or the sheer inability to pay regular rents keep adults constantly on the move and send kids reeling from place to place throughout their adolescence, never giving them a chance to put down roots and make permanent friends. Schools are criticized all over the country for failing the students they should be helping. Crime casts a shadow over every household, and crimes specifically against kids—from the resurgence of gang warfare to hunting them down for their hundred-dollar running shoes or designer clothing—are on the rise.

Parents have fallen victim to the same stresses. Millions of adults have alcohol or drug problems of their own, trapping their children in their misery. Emotional and physical abuse of children by parents is all too common.

Alcohol and other drugs can't solve these problems, but they can blot them out and make them seem very far away and unimportant. The worse the problem, the more drugs may seem necessary. Drugs are reliable; unlike parents, they are always there. Drugs also provide the perfect excuse for kids who feel guilty about not being able to solve their problems. Someone who is stoned can't be expected to change the world. Parents who use drugs to avoid their problems leave a doubly harmful legacy to their children.

Often when children say that they are using drugs just to feel good, their real reasons may lie deeper, possibly hidden even to themselves. These are the underlying reasons that good therapy can and must reveal if the rehab is to do any good.

The great developmental psychologists of history have all stressed how important the adolescent years are in turning a selfish child into a responsible adult. During those years adolescents must learn how to separate their identities from those of their parents while still maintaining a feeling of belonging with them. They must learn how to form and live up to their commitments and responsibilities. They must take the values they learned as children and test them against the changing world to form value systems of their own. Experimentation and rebellion must be part of all these processes, a major reason why the adolescent years can be so traumatic and painful. Drugs may be seen as a way of avoiding the pain, a continuation of the pleasures of childhood. But this is not an escape. It is a trap.

Doing drugs to blot out reality is extremely dangerous. Reality never disappears. At most, it can be evaded for a little while. By not confronting reality, the drug users slips into a vicious cycle in which the drugs themselves may be making worse the problem they are intended to avoid.

Drug use to escape reality almost always winds up in Stage 3 or 4 unless intervention is successful and the root cause exposed and dealt with. Without intervention, the pressures and the addiction may become overwhelming. Suicide is the ultimate escape. Thousands of youth attempt it even without an addiction to drugs. The combination of escape and drugs has killed many and will kill thousands more.

5. Escape from internal emotional problems. Kids do rise from poverty, single parents do marry and form stable homes, lost youth do make friends or find inspirational teachers. The world around us changes rapidly. Most youth find that the passage of time by itself solves many of their problems.

Children with emotional problems, however, may feel at a loss to cope even with the normal trials of life. These children may be especially susceptible to the lure of drugs. Researchers have studied what puts children at risk for drugs. Two patterns stand out. One is a lack of the many skills needed for dealing with others. The other pattern is related to their emotions. As Dr. Donald Macdonald writes, "Drug use produces low self- esteem, and low self-esteem promotes drug use." Children susceptible to drug problems were also found to be typically lonely, feeling as if they were not a part of their world, simply did not belong. Perhaps as a result of this, their wants and needs were jumbled together. Their needs may have been for discipline, a sense of place, the feeling of worthiness. Instead, their wants made them focus on one thing that would apparently make these problems fade into a manageable back-ground—drugs.

The variety of drugs gives these children almost a supermarket of choice to combat not just low self-esteem, but also shyness, anxiety, depression and a host of other problems. Alcohol sometimes breaks down inhibitions and turns the shy youngster into the life of the party. Cocaine provides arrogance and the feeling of power. PCP makes the user feel invincible. Marijuana banishes tension and makes the world mellow and dreamy. LSD opens eyes to a new reality. For any problem a child can suffer, there is the lure of a drug to make troubles vanish for as long as the drug is in the body.

Dealing with emotional problems by means of drugs is a sure way to dive into Stage 3 or 4 behavior very quickly. The colorful haze of drugs will beat the icy blackness of reality every time. Drugs create a new set of problems, though, and these will intertwine with the already existing ones until only the best-trained therapists can tell them apart.

We don't expect you to make those distinctions. If you observe problems of this magnitude in your children, seek help whether you think drugs are involved or not. If this book helps you to understand that drugs may be part of the problem, then you're a step ahead. But whether those problems come from drugs or from other ills is less important than intervening before they grow too severe. Suicide is all too often the last resort of kids whose internal problems prove overwhelming.

One final reason. Weaving in and out of every category we've listed is a reason so basic, so much a part of every single thing that children do, that it has to be singled out on its own so that no one can pretend to ignore it. Here it is:

A main reason kids use drugs is because adults use drugs.

That's it, short and simple. Kids imitate adults, and adults use drugs. If we were asked what predicts drug use better than any other sign, we would just ask, Do you use them yourself? If so, then your children will probably at least try them.

Now this isn't a hard-and-fast rule. Some children of users get so disgusted that they will never use drugs themselves; teetotalers' children can rebel and become heavy drug users. But before you look to your children, look to yourself.

And we're going beyond today's knowledge that there is a genetic component to alcoholism, that the children of alcoholics are much more likely to become alcoholics themselves. We're talking about your behaviors. Do you get drunk or high where your children can see you? Do you reach for a beer or mix a drink when you get home from a hard day at work? Do you smoke cigarettes to keep tensions down? Do you think a party is dull if no booze is available? Are sports an occasion for putting away a six-pack or two? Do you think it's cute to order a fake cocktail for your child at a restaurant? Do you start your children on alcohol or marijuana at home so they'll learn what it's all about? Do you pop speed or caffeine pills to be able to drive longer and farther during a vacation? Do you grow marijuana or leave drug paraphernalia in plain sight? Have your kids ever walked into a party and seen you snorting coke? If so, you may be teaching your child to use drugs.

Kids learn drug behavior from adults. Adults teach that prescription medications promise to eliminate pain, erase anxiety and make sleep come easier. Alcohol is the lubricant of the social bond. Speed uplifts college student brains to allow them to pull all-nighters before final exams. Steroids turn average athletes into extraordinary ones. Far too many adults teach that a magic potion exists for every conceivable ailment.

Condoning drug use around the house is as dangerous as condoning the "do-drug" society we have built. Tobacco ads, banned from television, appear instead in magazines oriented toward adolescents. Movies show a constant stream of attractive characters who drink, smoke or use other drugs. Beer commercials on television portray young, happy people drinking to achieve that good time. In fact, one estimate places the number of television commercials for alcohol that a child sees by age 18 at 100,000.

We'll return to parents' drug attitudes in Chapter 12, because they are so absolutely crucial to whether and how children use drugs. We just want to leave you with one thought: If you want to stop drug use in your children, first stop it in yourself.

5

Denial and Enabling

I f your children are doing drugs, you're probably helping them.
We don't say you're helping them consciously: You may be entirely unaware that they're doing drugs at all. That's part of the problem. Kids can't get away with doing drugs unless their parents either are able to blind themselves to the truth or know the facts but are backing off from a confrontation. The first is called denial, and the second is enabling.

Denial is the inability to see the harmful consequences of drinking or using other drugs. Enabling is supporting someone by not allowing that person to confront the consequences of drinking or other drug use. Both parents and kids practice denial, but enabling is much more often a parent's role.

Parental denial has been described as an adult drug. Like a drug it is seductive and comforting, a means of evading the stresses and pains of the real world. Even now many of you will try to deny or minimize the extent of your children's involvement with drugs. You'll want to believe your kids when they deny drug use. They know this, and they'll take advantage of it. They'll do this partly because they don't want to get caught but also partly because kids won't admit to themselves that drugs are as bad for them as parents say. And they get away with it solely because their parents actually help them to do so with their enabling. Let's look at each in turn.

Parental Denial

Denial is not a simple process. It can be as deeply layered as an onion, because the problems and the pains caused by your children's drug use are also multi-layered. We will try to peel back these layers and show you how denial can disrupt your thinking, starting with the most basic aspect of denial: the denial of an unpleasant truth.

Denial That Your Kids Are Using Drugs

If you're a parent, you've heard a lot about drugs, seen the headlines in the newspaper, watched the specials on television, attended meetings at your local schools. You surely know by now that junior high and even elementary school kids are using drugs and that regular drug use strikes every kind of family in every neighborhood. No matter, if you're like many parents, you'll shut down your suspicions about your own kids' involvement with drugs until the evidence is overwhelming.

Tim has a story to tell about a parent who was all too typically blind:

A father called me in one day and told me he thought his son was dealing marijuana. I asked him what the clues were, and he told me that his son had bought himself a water bed, stereo and new car, but he didn't have a job. I told him those were pretty obvious clues and asked if he had even more. He said yes, his son had a padlock on his bedroom door. This infuriated me. My house will never have a lock on any inside door: If one appears, it will be exploded off in a matter of seconds. With the father's permission, I cut the padlock off and searched the room. Paraphernalia was visible everywhere. The marijuana was all the way down in the crawl space stapled to the roof rafters. Sometimes it's really tough to find the drugs. But you don't need to find the drugs to figure out that there is a problem and deal with it.

Written out like this, the signs are unmistakable. To a father inside the situation, a father who desperately wanted not to believe that his son was dealing drugs, the evidence was suspect. There had to be another answer. This is denial.

Why do parents deny? One major reason is that it's almost impossible for parents to have a good relationship with their children unless they offer support and trust, not disbelief and punishment. Parents express support through a thousand daily incidents: helping a child overcome fears on the first day of school, teaching that child how to ride a bicycle, nursing him or her through sicknesses and injuries. As a parent you've always been on your children's side, right or wrong. You believe what they tell you, taking their side against a teacher whom they accuse of treating them unfairly, against a neighbor whose child they say started a fight. Most parents see this as their role. Asking them to stop believing their children when drugs are involved strikes them as a betrayal. But what parents fail to understand is that by using drugs, their children have already violated their parents' trust.

To get past denial, parents need to be educated. What we've tried to do in this book is to make parents as knowledgeable about drugs as their kids already are. In the past, parents have been conned by their own children who knew that they could tell lies because their parents didn't want to know the truth and wouldn't be able to tell the truth from lies even if they did. Tim defines it by saying that:

Denial is a result of parents' lack of knowledge and understanding of alcohol and drug use: how their kids use drugs and why, what the drugs look like, what paraphernalia is used, what the drug dealers tell their children and, most of all, the things about drugs that their children believe are true. Kids know that parents are ignorant about drugs and use that ignorance to their utmost advantage.

Ask yourself if you've ever heard any of these lines:

▼ "It's the chlorine in the school pool that's giving me red eyes."
▼ "I'm only keeping those drugs for a friend. I'd never use them myself."
▼ "I know it's late but the car broke down and we weren't near a phone so I couldn't call."
▼ "I did try drugs once but it made me so sick that I'll never do it again."

These are most likely the statements of children trying to slip excuses past parents who are desperately hoping for reasons to deny their rightful suspicions. Swallowing your children's excuses even as they grow more transparent and unbelievable is not helping them. Denial just prolongs drug use, exactly the opposite of what parents should want.

Denial That Drugs Are Really a Problem

For many parents, getting past their denial is not a single step, but a series of hurdles they must overcome. First comes making the admission that a child has used drugs. The usual next phase is to get past denying that the problem is major.

Drugs, not a major problem? Though put that way it sounds ridiculous, for most Americans drugs are somebody else's problem, not something that could happen in their own house.

Think about what we've said about drugs in American society. In millions of homes parties, sporting events and picnics aren't complete without alcohol. Large numbers of people who grew up in the 1960s still consider marijuana to be a positive alternative to hard liquor. Until a few years ago, even cocaine was proclaimed to be relatively harmless. As long as adults continue to have these attitudes, they will minimize the potential harm that drugs pose for their kids. Here are more classic phrases, this time ones used by parents:

- ▼ "I only caught them with beer, not hard liquor."
- ▼ "At least it was only alcohol and not drugs."
- ▼ "There's no real problem because there's no trouble in school."
- ▼ "They're only doing it at home, not hanging out with a bunch of bad kids."
- ▼ "Hey, they're not doing any more than I did when I was a kid and I turned out all right."

If any of these phrases sound familiar, you need to change your thinking. All drugs, alcohol very much included, are dangerous for kids. Allowing kids to drink or use drugs at home in the misguided feeling that you're keeping an eye on them is enabling. The drugs that kids are using today—often many times more potent and laced with poisons to give them even more kick—bear little resemblance to the ones used by earlier generations. Worse, where first experimentation used to be a beer or a joint in the mid-teens, today's youth are starting their exploration of drugs in grammar school, and preteen alcoholics and crack addicts have appeared.

Kids who use any drugs at all, including alcohol, have a problem. Parents should not excuse, dismiss or minimize this problem. Drug use is a crisis, and not just for the user but for the whole family—which brings us to one more major area of denial.

Denial That Drugs Affect the Entire Family

When a child is dependent on alcohol, drugs or both, all the other family members are affected, even the youngest. Drug abuse throws the family out of balance by creating stress and tension. Each family member has to learn how to adapt and survive. This is hardest on the other kids in the household. Often they are afraid to talk about what they think is happening; sometimes the changes take place so gradually that no one can determine what caused the way they feel. Kids whose siblings are on drugs learn very quickly not to talk about or confront their feelings if they see their parents denying obvious drug use. Just as it is true that parents who use drugs teach their kids to use drugs, parents who deny teach their kids denial.

And what more could a drug-using child hope for than denial? The more denial, the more drugs that child can get away with. Driving a wedge between parents is almost as useful. And while parents are practicing denial or looking the other way, the drug user will also likely get brothers or sisters involved in drugs. Even if they resist, the problems and pain caused by siblings' drug use is going to affect their lives just as greatly. Let's look at each of these in turn.

Parenting should be equal work for the mother and father, but it rarely is. In many couples, one parent—usually but not always the mother— has an active involvement in the parenting, while the other withdraws from responsibility. When a Caretaker and a Withdrawer have a kid on drugs, denial can destroy the marriage and the household.

Normally all the work, blame, pain and guilt of dealing with a child on drugs fall onto the shoulders of the Caretaker. The Caretaker's role in the household is to ensure that nothing goes wrong and that the outside world sees only a happy, normal family. Having a kid on drugs destroys this image. Caretakers will cover up problems, bail the kids out of scrapes and neglect the other members of the family in an ever-spreading pattern of denial. A Withdrawer, on the other hand, denies that anything is wrong by refusing to take part in investigating or punishing. Withdrawers spend long hours at work or at church or social groups just to stay out of the way. This throws even more of the burden on the Caretaker. Parents can break under this kind of pressure; families can split up.

The surest way to wind up with two drug-using kids in a family is to start with one. As we've already said, drug users find younger brothers and sisters a resource for buying drugs so they can support their own habits. Siblings who use drugs are now equally guilty, making them less likely to snitch to their parents.

Second Users, as they're known, have their own reasons for trying drugs. Drug use, with its aura of rebellion, pleasure and independence, looks good to kids. If they see an admired older sibling using drugs—and getting away with it—there seems little reason for them not to join in on what they see as the good times. Now families have double trouble. If parents don't acknowledge that the older kid is using drugs, then for sure they'll deny that the younger, more "innocent" one is.

It's not inevitable that every child in a family will start using drugs: Kids are simply too different from one another to respond to problems in the same way. What is typical is for parents to put too much emphasis on the kid using drugs while not paying sufficient attention to their other children. Unable to see that they have allowed one child to disrupt the entire household, these parents fail to understand what the drug user is putting his or her siblings through. Drugs often bring other problems into a home: threats, squabbling, school and legal problems, thievery, late-night fights and trips to the emergency room. Even the kids who hold out and don't ever try drugs may find their lives in shambles.

These kids are often the ones most hurt by their siblings' behaviors. And parents exhausted from trying to deal with the problem kids won't be able to help them cope. As long as drug use isn't confronted, as long as parents try to deny what is happening in their homes, these non-using kids are the innocent victims.

Recognizing and confronting drug use at its first signs, making your other children aware of the pain and problems of drug use and not giving in to the temptation to smooth the troubled road ahead for the drug users are the best and only ways of keeping the rest of your family healthy and trouble-free.

User Denial

All drug users practice denial. Anti-drug messages flood our world, and users can no more escape them than they can avoid breathing. To continue using their drugs, they have to deny to themselves the truth of these messages. From the first sip or puff or snort, users somehow manage to cast a rosy and positive glow over what they're doing. Harm doesn't come into the picture. Adults try drugs because they are convinced they'll get something good out of the experience—fun times, peer acceptance, an end to boredom, relief from stress.

Kids are no different (see Chapter 4). In fact, they simply have more to deny. Not only do they have to deny the consequences of drug use, they have to somehow convince their watchful parents that they're not doing drugs at all. (Not to mention the law: Many kids are more scared of the police than they are of parents. And never forget that for those under the legal age, even alcohol and tobacco are illicit.)

The basic progression of user denial follows the stages we introduced in Chapter 2. It goes:

Stage 1: I'm not doing anything.
Stage 2: I'm not doing anything wrong.
Stage 3: I'm not doing anything harmful.
Stage 4: I'm not doing anything else.

I'm Not Doing Anything

Drugs are wrong. Whatever else kids know about drugs, they know this—not because drugs are dangerous and addictive, but because they can land the kid in big trouble. So kids lie.

The conning behavior we talked about earlier stems from kids' need to deny their drug use. Our upcoming chapters on Red Flags are full of cons: the mouthwash to cover alcohol on the breath; incense to hide the smell of marijuana; invented sicknesses to mask drug-induced hangovers; lies about where kids are going, who they're seeing, what they're doing. These excuses are thin and easily seen through—except by parents practicing their own denial.

Fear of being caught and punished can keep this stage going long beyond the initial trials with drugs. Kids can develop elaborate double lives, presenting parents, teachers and other adults with a portrait of a "good," trouble-free youth while turning, like Dr. Jekyll and Mr. Hyde, into a druggie when only other druggies are around. For the youth it may seem like the best of both worlds. Not so. Leading a life of denial is stressful, and drug users under stress will turn to more drugs to free themselves for as long as they can stay high.

The rule is: Denial always leads to worse problems.

I'm Not Doing Anything Wrong.

Few kids genuinely like constant lying, so the need to do so sets up a pattern of denial and justification in their own heads. With kids on drugs, denial occurs automatically and unconsciously since they're forced to believe that what is false is actually true. They'll blame parents for forcing them to lie and rationalize the need to do so by insisting that drugs aren't evil. Parents' use of drugs reinforces this because then kids can accuse their parents of being hypocrites. Kids who use denial are not going to recognize the differences between what adults do and what children can't do.

Another popular rationalization is the hazy understanding kids have of drugs' positive role in medicine. Tim hears this one a lot:

> I talk to students throughout my state and they say, "Hey look, cancer patients use marijuana." They really believe that patients in hospitals put their feet up on the bed, kick back and reach over to a tray for a doobie, a marijuana cigarette. And then a nice-looking nurse comes over with a gold cigarette lighter and lights it up. Of course it's not true: Cancer patients get pills of synthetic THC, the active ingredient in marijuana. What the students never want to think of is the other ward

in the hospital, the one in which babies are born with birth defects because their mothers, some teen-aged, smoked marijuana or used other drugs during their pregnancies or may even have suffered genetic damage before they got pregnant.

Consequences don't mean much to kids. Adolescence is a time of risk taking and exploring as kids test limits—the limits of parental control, the limits of society's tolerance and the limits of nature and their own bodies. People often say that kids consider themselves immortal. That's not quite true: Today most kids know peers who have died, maybe in an alcohol-related crash, possibly by suicide. Kids just find it hard to make the mental leap that death is waiting for them as a result of their own actions. Drugs simply magnify the feeling that consequences happen to others, never to themselves. You can hear that attitude in these common phrases of kids who use denial:

▼ "I'm still doing well in school."
▼ "I only drink beer; I don't touch anything else."
▼ "Drugs make you more creative."
▼ "Drugs give you good times, not bad ones."
▼ "Parents don't remember what it's like to be a kid."

Kids have to lie about drugs: There's no way that they can use them otherwise. The real problem is that drugs eventually take over. As drug use progresses into Stage 3, the wrongness of drugs becomes a minor factor. Now kids have to assure themselves that they'll survive their drugs.

I'm Not Doing Anything Harmful

Most adolescents believe that they are simply too young to become alcoholic or drug dependent. They're dead wrong, of course. Drug counselors are now seeing kids under the age of 10 coming in with full-fledged addictions. Those kids became drug dependent through their own efforts. That there is no lower age limit for addiction is proved by the epidemic of babies being born with habits because of their mothers' use of alcohol or other drugs during pregnancy. Denial ensures not only that kids refuse to admit to themselves the simple fact of drugs' harmfulness but also that they will develop a stronger and more sophisticated defense system as the abuse and dependency continue.

Most kids are naturally optimistic: They look on the good side of life and forget the bad. Drugs reinforce this as well. Like adults, kids who get drunk at a party remember only the fun and laughter, not the late-night vomiting or the next-day hangover.

After a time, however, the downside of drugs becomes too frequent and too extensive to simply dismiss. At this point kids will often move to another stage of denial, minimizing the problem. They'll look at the drug world around them and find someone who is in worse shape and justify their own use by rationalizing that they're not as bad off, that they haven't crossed that imaginary line into worse horrors. They may say to themselves:

▼ "I can stop any time I want to."
▼ "I only party on weekends. I don't use drugs every day."
▼ "I just buy drugs for my own use. I don't sell them to others."
▼ "I just steal money from my mother. I don't sell my body to buy drugs."
▼ "I'm still alive. Drugs won't kill me."

They're wrong there, too. Drugs can kill them. True, very few kids get to that stage because it takes a tremendous amount of both denial and enabling on both sides to allow it to happen. When it does, it is next to impossible to keep users from the consequences of their behavior any longer.

I'm Not Doing Anything Else

As we said in Chapter 2, Stage 4 users require drugs just to feel normal. Nothing else in life really matters other than doing drugs and getting money, somehow, to pay for them. At this point, theft, assault, prostitution, drug dealing and a host of other problems become the norm.

Getting help to users at this point is extremely difficult. Kids' denial makes the parents' job harder. Parents will have had to put aside their denial by this stage, but they will still have to confront their child's denial in order to make that child understand that it is the drugs that are the real problem and the real danger to health. Adult addicts and alcoholics are notorious for not admitting their addictions until they hit bottom. Children are different. You can't sit back and wait for your child to reach that point. You have a responsibility to your children, and you have to live up to it. If not, you are enabling your children to continue their destruction.

Parents must recognize that the addiction is the primary disease. It is the issue that must be addressed *first*. Seek professional help from someone who is certified in alcohol and drug rehabilitation. There is no longer time for delay.

Enabling

Enabling grows out of the same protective instincts that bind parents to their children from the day their first child is born. Even after the facts of drug use become painfully clear, parental support will not suddenly disappear any more than the drug use will instantly vanish. Parents may see even more reason for support now than ever before: Users get themselves into continual problems. Very often parents will find it impossible to let their children suffer from problems, even the ones that they got themselves into. They enable their children, shielding them from the consequences of their own actions.

Parents enable out of guilt, fear and love for their children. It may seem crazy that parents who love their children will act in such a way that it actually keeps their children on drugs, but protecting their kids is so ingrained for some parents that it's impossible for them to stop and look objectively at what they are doing. We'll take a look at some aspects of enabling. Don't be surprised to see yourself in our descriptions.

Guilt

Too often, parents blame themselves for their children's behavior. Parents who feel guilty about not seeing enough of their kids because of the pressures of jobs, single parents who feel guilt because of their divorce, strict parents who feel that they've driven their kids into disobedience, lenient parents who feel they haven't laid down enough rules—almost all parents experience some particle of guilt that says, "If only I had done a better job."

Kids learn how to exploit their parents' guilt feelings. These parents may not be able to say no if their kids come home and say they want to have alcohol at their party. They may strike a bargain with their children that the kids can drink at home if only they don't do it anywhere else.

Parents deep into their own denial of drugs may feel the guilt of hypocrisy if they say no to their children trying the marijuana or cocaine they see their parents use. Similarly, parents whose own youth featured plenty of drugs and alcohol may feel that saying no would deprive their kids of a natural part of growing up. Parents who actively help to put their kids on drugs are the saddest and most destructive of all.

Kids are good at finding other ways of manipulating their parents, particularly by playing one parent off against the other. The mothers who worry because they can't be around in traditional homemaker roles and the fathers who shove money at their children in place of their time are ripe for exploitation. When the kid needs to be bailed out of a situation—for example, a citation for driving while impaired, being caught shoplifting, throwing up all over the new living room rug—these parents will run to their kids' rescue and get the mess cleaned up before the other parent can find out. They may tell themselves they're only trying to help their child, but they're really doing it to escape the guilt of not being the ideal parents they would like to be.

Certain parents also don't like to see their children too isolated or different from all others. If other parents allow their kids to smoke in the house, these parents will break down and let their child do so as well. If they know their kids are being shut out of their social circle by a too-strong parental stand on drugs, they'll relax their ideals so that their kids will fit in better.

All parents want a better life for their children. But standards are very important in turning a child into a healthy and responsible adult. The consequences of drugs are worse than whatever guilt you may suffer because of a child's momentary unhappiness. Drugs are never the answer, and parents should never feel guilty for standing up and saying no.

Fear

Kids don't look ahead to the long-term consequences of drug use. That's sad but to be expected: Kids don't look to the long term in much of anything. Parents aren't supposed to act so foolishly, but they do. And when their fear of the short-term consequences is greater than their fear of drugs, they enable.

Many parents are deathly afraid of losing control over their kids. Rather than worrying that their children might be using drugs outside the home and out of their control, some parents allow their kids to keep beer in the kitchen refrigerator or borrow from the liquor cabinet or smoke pot in their rooms. They'd rather send the message that drugs are okay than lose authority by not knowing what their kids are doing.

Other parents are simply afraid of their kids and have already lost control of their behavior. These parents back down from challenges. If they hear their child say, "I'm not using drugs," they'll believe the statement no matter what the evidence. If their children warn them to stop their nagging or they'll do even more drugs, the parents will keep quiet. If their kid comes home drunk and belligerent, these parents will turn their head rather than start a fight. If they have an older child on drugs and running wild, they'll pretend that nothing is wrong for fear of having that child move out of the house.

Many parents desperately try to keep their children's problems safely tucked away in the home and rush to protect them when the outside world wants them punished. These parents fear that would happen if their children were to be expelled from school or develop police records and so work their hardest to cover for their kids.

Enabling parents may start with little things, like telling teachers that their children were home sick instead of admitting that they were suffering from a hangover or a drug binge. Later these same parents may shop around for new schools for their children rather than let them be stigmatized as problem children. Outside of school they'll pay off insurance claims for car crashes or hire expensive lawyers to clear their children's records from charges of shoplifting or DUI.

Enabling parents simply don't understand that they are only delaying the inevitable—and that the more they delay, the worse the consequences will be when their children finally have to face up to themselves and their actions.

Love

Parents go through life wishing they could take away all their children's ills and hurts. Parents kiss away the pain from a scraped arm after a fall off a bicycle and stay up nights with the child suffering from chicken pox. Any person who doesn't act in this way is deemed unfit to be a parent. The problem is that most parents carry this behavior over to the way they treat their children's drug use.

We understand how difficult it is for parents to watch their loved ones get hurt. Because of the very nature of addiction, alcoholics and addicts do not see their own dependency, no matter how clear it might be to their families. Out of love, parents will enable their children's addictions, meaning that the addiction progresses without proper intervention. Allowing alcoholics and addicts to experience their own problems helps them to hit their bottom, forcing them to let reality penetrate their wall of denial.

Others Who Enable

Parents aren't the only ones who enable. Siblings will cover up for their brothers and sisters; friends will spur one another to use drugs; teachers will overlook obvious drug problems; police will let kids go as a favor to the family. Sometimes the entire world seems as if it's in a conspiracy to encourage kids to use drugs, teach them that drug use is really positive and shield them from the harm that drugs can do.

The "do-drug" message that we've talked about earlier is really a form of societal enabling. True, bits of this are slowly changing: On television today it's usually the bad guys who smoke cigarettes, drug humor is mostly forbidden and characters don't spend as much time drinking as they once did.

Still, alcohol and drugs are very much a part of our society. Beer commercials with their message that good times require alcohol play to younger and younger audiences. Romance magazines aimed at teenage girls come stuffed with color cigarette ads. Athletes get second and third chances to return to their teams and their huge salaries after testing positive for drugs. Canadian Olympic sprinter Ben Johnson, stripped of his gold medal because of steroid use, was recently offered the highest appearance fee ever for a track meet in his return to competition. The best-seller lists are filled with autobiographies of celebrities detailing their hidden lives as alcoholics and drug addicts. Sadly, the emphasis seems to be less on their newfound and hard-won freedom from drugs than on the glamorous lives they once lived while doing drugs.

Parents need to awaken themselves to the glamorization of drug use in our society, especially to the use of the licit gateway drugs, such as cigarettes and alcohol. Point out the mixed messages sent when the very names of athletic events contain a cigarette brand name, or when a rock concert tour by an alcoholic rock star is sponsored by a manufacturer of alcoholic beverages. Make note of the great number of times in movies or on television when alcohol or other drugs are depicted as being indispensable parts of good times or gracious living. Talk with your children whenever a newspaper or magazine article seems to suggest that pills are available to eliminate all our everyday problems.

Judging by the adulation given to celebrities who give up the use of drugs after many drug-filled years, our society has an unfortunate tendency to condone those who run wild in their youth, as long as they later reform. Possibly parents do this unconsciously, with memories of their own pasts ever-present in their minds. It would help if those who practice life-long virtues of chastity, abstinence and temperance were not so often characterized as prudes, prigs and goody-goodies.

It's too bad that no autobiographies can ever be forthcoming from the dead celebrities who overdosed, crashed their cars, choked to death on their vomit or committed suicide while on drugs. As long as examples from the glamorous living continue to overwhelm lessons from the silent dead, parents will have to work twice as hard in countering the drug-enabling message the media spews out.

We can only hope that parents use this chapter to force themselves to examine their own actions and behaviors. Denial and enabling allow your children to do drugs. If you want them to stop, you must change yourselves.

6

The Red Flags: Introduction

In the next five chapters we'll guide you through the skewed, bizarre, sometimes violent and usually pitiful world of users and abusers of alcohol and other drugs.

Out of Tim's experience through his years working with youth—both as a detective and in face-to-face encounters in dozens of high schools and colleges—and from the writings of other noted experts we've pulled together more than 200 Red Flags of drug use and abuse. Red Flags are more than symptoms yet certainly not absolute proof. We call them Red Flags for a purpose: They are warnings to parents that something is wrong with their children.

The Red Flags

Parents can't help noticing changes in their children when kids use alcohol or other drugs. Most parents, though, not looking specifically for drugs, will find it difficult to put their finger on exactly what is bothering them. Many of the changes are quite subtle; others come on extremely suddenly. Certain clues will simply be baffling to or go completely unobserved by parents unfamiliar with the effects of drugs. Our Red Flags are designed to translate your feelings of unease into words and to make clear the warning signs of drug use.

As we list more than 200 Red Flags covering virtually every aspect of a child's life, we understand that their sheer number may appear overwhelming. Fortunately, they fall into a number of patterns and groupings, which we've carefully sorted to make them easier for you to understand. This is the largest and most comprehensive list of Red Flags to be found anywhere: If your child is on drugs, he or she is certain to exhibit some Red Flag behavior.

Note: Whenever we refer to "drugs" or "drug use," we refer to all conceivable drugs, including alcohol. It is extremely important that parents remember this as they read the chapters on Red Flags.

Red Flags fall into five major groupings, which we have placed in separated chapters, each highlighting a different aspect of drug-induced consequences.

❖ Chapter 7: Changes in Personality

Drugs not only alter personality traits—loss of motivation is an all-too-typical change—but will also worsen any personality problems that may have led the child to take the drugs in the first place, such as low self-esteem or a lack of maturity. Kids know that drugs are wrong and that they must hide their use, so they are forced to lie and defend their behavior. Relationships change and crumble as denial and paranoia take over users' lives. At the end lies violence, to others and to themselves.

❖ Chapter 8: Changes in Activities and Habits

Often parents can see changes more objectively in *how* their children behave than in *who* they are. Drugs can alter the most basic elements in users' lives, from their sleeping and eating patterns to their values and beliefs. Old friends and activities will be discarded as drugs come to dominate lives and users seek out others like themselves. Problems may often show up most clearly outside the home, at school or work where teachers and employees—more objective even than parents—are less easy to manipulate.

❖ Chapter 9: Changes in Physical Appearance

Not only can drugs affect overall physical development and health, but their use also leaves behind a number of telltale signs on the body. Eyes, mouth, nose, skin, speech and movement all can be watched for tangible evidence of drug use.

❖ Chapter 10: Paraphernalia

Pipes and needles are obvious indicators of drug use. Ingenious children, however, have discovered ways to turn even the most innocuous household objects, from pop cans to toilet paper rolls, into tools for drug use.

❖ Chapter 11: Legal Problems

Drug use can bring users into conflicts with the authorities. Drugs and driving lead inevitably to citations and crashes. Needing drug money, users may steal, attack others or sell their possessions or bodies for drugs. Finally, drugs can lead to rage and violence. If drugs were removed from society, crime would plummet.

Looking for the Pattern

There is no one right way—and certainly no single Red Flag—that parents can use to tell if their children are using alcohol or other drugs. Even if a child is caught red-handed using drugs, parents will find it difficult to ascertain what stage a child is in unless they look at the overall pattern of Red Flags that their child displays.

Because we've grouped the Red Flags into chapters, parents can search for a pattern in a number of different ways. The Red Flags in Chapters 9 and 10, on physical signs and paraphernalia, are often tied to individual drugs. Parents can use these to gain a sense of what drugs their children are using, to what extent and for how long. Parents should not let a quest for a specific drug blind them, however: Few regular drug users stop at one drug. Many users sample a wide variety of drugs and turn from one to another if the other one happens to be more available or seems more interesting at the moment; this can possibly result in the user becoming cross-addicted or a polyuser.

In the long run, kids who are on marijuana or alcohol or crack or any combination of these will exhibit many of the same behaviors. The essential fact that a child is on drugs is enough to account for most emotional and behavioral changes that parents will see. Parents should first cut through their denial and convince themselves that their child is using drugs; knowing which drug (or drugs) can come later and be part of the intervention and rehabilitation process.

A single Red Flag may not necessarily indicate drug use. Parents who see their children displaying several Red Flags from a single chapter have much more powerful evidence of drug use. And parents who find their children displaying many Red Flags scattered throughout more than one chapter should take immediate steps to investigate whether that child is on drugs—by confronting the child, searching for hidden drugs or paraphernalia, or monitoring the child's behavior—or if drugs are exacerbating other serious problems.

Trust

Trust is a bond between parent and child. Most parents trust their children to behave properly and make the right decisions for themselves; most children trust their parents to allow them to grow and mature with guidance.

But many parents and children fail to realize that trust must be earned. We are at our babies' side holding their hand as they learn to walk and to climb stairs. With time they earn our trust to do it by themselves, even if that means they occasionally fall. Handing children trust is like handing them your car keys without ever first riding along with them. Trust can't be handed over blindly. When children don't come through, they don't deserve complete trust until they can prove their proper behavior. Some people call this "tough love."

Parents may wonder how to square being on the lookout for so many tiny clues of possible drug-influenced behavior with trusting their children. Let's deal with some hypothetical questions from parents on what the Red Flags mean.

Doesn't a constant watch for Red Flags turn us into spies on our own home?

As parents, you've been watching over your children since the day they were born. You've checked them to make sure their diapers didn't need changing, that they've done their homework, that their rooms are properly picked up. You've felt their forehead for fevers and checked their cheeks for spots. You are no more spies when you look for signs of alcohol or other drug use than when you watch out for any other illness or problem.

Our Red Flags are there just to help you make sense of problems that you may already be seeing—possibly without understanding what these actions truly represent.

How can we have trust in our children if we're to be suspicious of every move they make?

Kids will test the bounds that their parents place on them. Parents have a right to tighten those bounds if children abuse their trust. If you tell a child to be home by 11:00 on a Saturday night, you'll be rightfully angry if that child stays out until 11:30. The next Saturday you may again trust your child to be home by 11:00—but you'll be checking your watch as well.

Parents who have been working to educate their children about drugs and create a drug-free atmosphere in their home, as we specify in Chapter 12, can allow their children the room to grow and mature without constant supervision. But a child whose behavior runs up several Red Flags has already broken the bounds of trust and must be treated differently than children you believe to be drug-free. A pattern of Red Flag behavior should serve as a signal that you've been missing a problem that already exists. Knowledge of problem behavior gives parents the right to be aware of the cause of that behavior. When it comes to drugs, parents have no choice but to be on the lookout and act immediately.

Observing Red Flag Behavior

Now, please carefully read the next five chapters and try to relate them to your children's lives. Remember, you should usually be looking especially for sudden and extreme changes: those are most likely to stem from recent involvement in drugs. We build on the material presented in Chapters 2–5. If you have any questions, you might want to go back and reread those to understand what we mean when we mention drug stages, denial and enabling, reasons for use or specific drugs.

Under each heading inside a chapter, we group a number of Red Flags that either are directly related or provide similar clues to behavior. We also provide cross-references when another side of the same Red Flag behaviors can be found in a different chapter. You should assume that the Red Flags within a chapter are highly interrelated.

Please don't try to pick and choose among the Red Flags. Check them all: They may provide keys to your children's attitudes and appearances that you have never closely examined. Any one of them may spark recognition in your eyes.

Note: It May Not Be Drugs

Most Red Flags are warnings of problems, not positive proof of drug use. Parents should be careful to not make specific accusations until they find a pattern of evidence in their child's behavior. As we detail in Chapter 12, no accusation should be made without presenting all the reasons that you think drugs are involved. You should not often be wrong, especially if your physical evidence is strong. Parents relying entirely on changes in personality or attitude, however, may mistake the symptoms of other ailments for drug use.

Both physical and psychological illnesses can produce symptoms that closely mimic those stemming from drugs. Divorce, alcoholic or drug-using parents, poverty, frequent moves, neglect or abuse can create such serious emotional stress that many Red Flags become apparent. For some youth, just the everyday pressure of adolescence can produce a crisis.

If your child convinces you beyond the possibility of a doubt that he or she is not using drugs, you still have a child with a serious problem. Getting a competent professional to assess your child could be crucial. In addition to any effects from the ailment itself, children with unresolved major problems are at high risk of turning to drugs for escape or release. Even problems not complicated by drugs today could become so in the future. If you let this occur, the drugs will both worsen the initial problem and create a delay in confronting and solving it.

Parents should never assume that drugs are the cause of their children's behaviors—nor ever rule them out entirely. Treat each case as unique, and do what is best for that child without preconceived notions.

7

Red Flags: Changes in Personality

Drugs can alienate your children from you. Strong words, but true. The child you once knew may be replaced by a surly, solitary, uncooperative, possibly violent drug user. While personality changes will vary with the child, in almost all cases these changes are progressive: The heavier the involvement with drugs and/or the later the stage of use that the child is in, the more extreme the changes in that child's personality.

Living with a child on drugs is not at all easy. No matter what crises his or her behavior may provoke, a child full of drug denial may not even admit that problems exist. Children on alcohol or other drugs often experience sudden mood swings, and thus parents may never know which mood to expect. Whether parents try to minimize problems through enabling and denial or whether there are constant stormy battles, other children in the household are going to be hurt as their parents' energies become focused on the drug user. Hurt and neglected, siblings are then also at risk for drugs.

While a few drugs can cause almost instantaneous mood swings in a user, most of the personality changes we discuss in this chapter take longer to develop and are directly related to the stage of drug use that the child is in. Even so, these changes will come on faster than the gradual shifts in personality that non–drug-using children experience as they grow from preteens to college age.

Parents should try to pinpoint just when they first started noticing these changes in their youngsters so that they have clues as to the duration of serious drug use. Many parents find that it builds their confidence to confirm that others see the same problems in their children. Outsiders—friends, relatives, teachers, clergy—sometimes can spot these changes more easily than do parents, who see their children every day. The fact that changes are obvious and noticeable lends weight to the inevitable confrontation with the child.

Personality Shifts

Sudden general personality changes
Mood swings in short periods of time
More irritable; secretive; unpredictable; hostile; depressed; uncoopera-
     tive; apathetic; withdrawn; sullen; easily provoked; oversensitive; de-
     fensive; nervous; ambivalent; anxious; forgetful
Less affectionate; caring; helpful; loving

One of the marvelous things about babies is that a distraction can shift them from an all-out cry to a smile in a second. Babies do this absolutely naturally: The everyday joys and wonders of life are so powerful that they can override discomfort and pain. Unfortunately for parents who want their sleep, these moods can switch back just as fast.

What is attractive in an infant is serious in an adolescent. Drugs can turn your children into emotional babies. Admittedly, parents of teenagers may on occasion think this is true in any case: Adolescence is naturally a period of emotional ups and downs in which good times seem more wonderful, minor problems more devastating than at any later time of life. But non–drug-using children are naturally resilient. No matter how bad the momentary crisis, they will normally swing back to an equilibrium.

This is not so with children whose emotions are being driven by drugs. Children who spend much of their lives at extreme highs and lows may be suffering from a serious illness, such as manic-depressive psychosis, but are much more likely to be driven by the raging pressures of the drugs within them. Kids on drugs will react turbulently to the same outside stresses as non–drug-using kids, perhaps more so, and they will also change moods for no reason at all.

Exactly how your child might change is something we can't predict. To give you an idea of what to look for we've listed in the Red Flags above 20 behaviors and emotions that kids on drugs are known to exhibit. When these are sudden, unpredictable and frequent, you need to start thinking of drugs as their cause.

Long-term changes also occur, in part because drug use retards emotional development in a youngster. Users generally become more distant and less affectionate to those they were once close to. They are so sensitive that the rest of the family must be careful what they say. Confrontation will provoke hostility and defensiveness.

Many children on drugs will become solitary and withdrawn, even ones who had been outgoing and gregarious. A sad change common to many drug users is that they no longer seem as sharp mentally as before—they begin to have lapses in memory. Users' priorities change as drugs take over their lives, and these are reflected in their attitudes to the world around them.

Lack of Maturity

Emotional and social immaturity
Needs instant gratification
Tunnel vision—narrow attitude on problems and solutions
Emotional growth is suspended

Maturity may be characterized in many ways: the ability to understand and interact with other people; feelings of selflessness and concern about others; the ability to defer immediate pleasures for future good. Drugs negate all of these.

Drugs focus attention on the "I." Users' concerns are solely for themselves and their own immediate enjoyment. Once past the early, social stages, drug use is an end in itself: The object is to get high and stay high by whatever means are necessary.

The negative personality traits that drugs provoke—the paranoia about dealing with non–drug users, the destruction of family relationships—all tend to bring a child's emotional development to a halt. Kids heavily using drugs not only will be mentally less acute than other kids but will also appear less mature, unable to gain the perspective on problems needed to solve them. It's a double whammy that spreads into every facet of their lives, leading them to drop out of school, lose jobs, abandon friends and family. If your child has stopped growing up, drugs may well be the cause.

Parents/Family Relationships

Resists or breaks family rules
Refuses to talk to parents about problems
Refuses to talk to parents at all
Changes in family relationships
Increasing conflict with parents or siblings
Increasing isolation from family

Refuses to introduce friends to parents

Drugs ruin family relationships. The user's personality shifts may eventually force you to deal with a stranger in your own house. Worse, that stranger is only a child, one who knows that his or her behavior is wrong and has to be hidden from parents, creating more guilt and more stress.

As parents you'll surely notice these changes taking place. Getting your children to talk about them will be much more difficult. Drug-using kids are very resistant about communicating with their parents. In many cases they'll simply shut down, refusing to talk about anything that is going on in their lives. Part of this is the guilt and paranoia of the drug user.

Another major problem comes from the feelings of specialness that users develop, the notion that only other users can truly understand what they are experiencing. Drug users may start spending more time with other drug users, whom they'll keep as far away from their parents as possible. Parents should be suspicious of friends who just honk the horn or refuse to come into the house when picking up their kids. These kids are trying to avoid established authority—parents—for fear that their drug use will be detected.

Friends/Relationships

Increasing hang-ups in close relationships, especially with close friends or in sexual relationships

Decreasing interest in non–drug-using friends

Makes friends who are also loners

Defends drug use by friends

Makes all new friends who are older, strange-looking or clearly drug-using

A sudden shift away from a child's current friends, especially to older kids, is a strong signal that drugs are involved.

Youth like to hang around with others who have the same interests and attitudes. Drugs become a bond that take over users' lives. Users reject the normal world. Non–drug-using friends are felt to be "out of touch" or "chicken." Their inability to handle drugs is looked down on by the users. Relationships with other children are likely to be limited to sharing drugs or trading favors for drugs. The delicate interplay of learning about dating, love and sex may be derailed by drug use.

Rejection because of drugs works both ways. The same moodiness and selfishness that causes rifts with parents will alienate even the closest friends. Destructive verbal and physical behavior caused by drugs—crashing parties, stealing from friends, damaging borrowed cars—is also a barrier to social acceptance. The only way users can recover lost growth and regain abandoned friends is to tackle their emotional development problems in the recovery process after the drug abuse has ended.

Lack of Desire

Decreasing interest in learning anything new
General passive attitude
Loses interest in school, sports and hobbies
Loses initiative

Loss of desire is now known to be such a major indicator of long-term drug use that it has been given a formidable scientific name: "amotivational syndrome." Amotivational syndrome is often associated with marijuana use, but it can also occur as a result of the use of other drugs.

The drive to grow, to learn new things, explore new ideas, solve problems, change—these should be a basic underpinning of the adolescent years. Drugs dampen these desires and cause goals to recede and change to become threatening. Kids on drugs feel that their world is okay the way it is, even if to all outside appearances they are suffering. Not only does the desire to learn become almost nonexistent, but the material that is learned takes much longer to grasp as well. Users find that it's harder for them to hang on to that knowledge and retain it for future use. (See also Chapter 8, "School-Related Problems.")

Lack of motivation isn't limited just to schoolwork. Loss of initiative makes activities that once seemed all-consuming—hobbies, sports, careers—take a back seat. While kids often casually abandon interests, non–drug-using children usually quickly replace them with new ones. Indications that a child has stopped caring about former activities may be a signal that drug use has turned to abuse or that it has progressed to a later stage.

Parents should take note when their children quit their former activities, especially if they pick up a new set of friends in the process. Unless the child can get off drugs, this lack of desire will overwhelm anything a parent can do to try to make a difference. A common phrase heard from users is "you don't understand," and this is probably true. Those not on drugs will find it hard to understand their effects, but drug changes should be plain to see.

Low Self-Esteem

Develops feelings of hopelessness or helplessness
Suffers from guilt
Feels sad, hurt and frightened
Growing feelings of inferiority
Loses confidence in school
Becomes socially isolated and withdrawn
Drops out of sports and school activities

Estranged from friends, antagonistic to parents and family, isolated from old interests and activities, bored and doing poorly in school: Drug users may show a defiant face to the world but privately feel miserable and depressed. Kids suffering from low self-esteem are in a vicious cycle in which their very feelings of inferiority make it harder for them to make the changes needed to rejoin the world they abandoned.

Kids on drugs no longer feel comfortable or desire to be involved with groups or group activities. Damaged or nonexistent self-confidence leads them to prefer isolation, spending much of their time alone in the bedroom, basement or other rooms away from the rest of the family. When forced into a group activity, kids with self-esteem problems will separate themselves—splintering off into a corner or edge of the room. Kids who do spend time with others prefer hanging out with one person who shares their attitude.

As the addiction progresses, drug-using children fall deeper into the abyss of lost self-respect. They will even acknowledge this fact and openly degrade themselves in front of family or peers, by make statements such as "I'm worthless" or "I don't have it anymore." At this point the characteristic look of the late-stage drug user emerges: lack of personal hygiene, indifference to clothes and appearance. (See also Chapter 9, "Appearance/Hygiene.") Users take the easy road, set few or no goals and view the future pessimistically.

Denial

Total denial that drugs might be harmful
Blames others for own irresponsible actions
Points out others' faults
Talks about adults' bad habits
Defends rights of youth

Kids in denial are hell-bent on justifying their drug use with two—seemingly contradictory—defenses.

One defense is rejecting the idea that drug use is truly wrong or harmful. You'll hear the claim that the dangers of drugs are just hype: scares and lies out of proportion to the truth. Athletes, rock stars, actors and other celebrities who seem to live glamorous lives while admitting to drug use will be cited. Kids on drugs will insist that they won't become abusers or addicts, that the drugs they use are "soft" or "safe" and that they can stop anytime they want.

The other defense tacitly admits that drug use is wrong but justifies it by pointing to the behavior of others. You'll be told that drug use is normal and even expected. Parents' use of any drugs, even tobacco or occasional alcohol use, will be thrown back in their faces. Kids will remind their parents that they experimented with drugs in their youth and will claim the same "right" to make their own mistakes. "No one is perfect," users will say, "that's the way life is." All other faults they can find in their parents' lives or in the world will be used as an excuse to justify and minimize their own bad behavior. Kids who loudly proclaim their "rights" to do drugs are often really crying for help—although it will be very difficult to get the child to admit this.

Lying

Becomes good con artist
Always has excuse no matter what problem is
Gives only vague, nonspecific or evasive answers to questions about
    behavior

Lying to oneself about drugs is denial. Lying to others is just plain lying. Lies are a necessary part of the drug experience for abusers. Drugs are illicit and wrong: Even the most brazen kids, even those in homes where drug use is allowed, will display behaviors that they have to cover up. Users need to try to make parents believe that they've never used drugs, that they've stopped, that they're holding drugs for friends, that they're in places they're supposed to be rather than out doing drugs. When money and possessions start disappearing, they'll have an excuse, just as they will when they start failing in school or getting into trouble with the law. (See also Chapter 11, "Legal Problems.") Drugs put kids onto a tightrope of lies; parents need to be there when they fall off.

Lateness

Increasingly late for school or work
Increasingly late returning home when out
Makes excuses for coming home late
Occasionally loses sense of time

Part of users' constant lateness is related to the lying and covering up they need to do to hide their drug use. Kids can't admit they spent the night too drunk to drive home or that they stopped off on the way from school to smoke pot with a friend. Kids who are habitually late distance themselves from their parents and family. For parents not to directly confront this behavior shows that communication between parent and child is lacking.

There's another component to lateness that shows up in later stages of drug use: a decreasing awareness of the passage of time. (See also Chapter 8, "Unexplained Absences.") Late-stage kids literally have no realization of how late they are because they no longer measure and understand time in the way nonusers do. Without this awareness they are unable to see a problem, perceiving it as "no big deal." Tardiness just brings excuses: "I was only a few minutes late" or "This was the first time this week I was late." These will only increase with time. In some cases, being late will become the routine instead of the exception. Late-stage users feel no responsibility to be on time or to consider the feelings of those waiting for them. They see their behavior as normal and justifiable. At this point, a true time sense is not likely to return until the rehabilitation process.

Fear/Paranoia

Paranoia
Feelings of being picked on

Use of some of the more popular drugs, especially marijuana and cocaine, can leave users feeling that someone is out to get them or that something bad is going to happen. These feelings of paranoia in the common rather than the clinical sense of the word can also be a more general response to the fears of being caught doing something drug users know to be very wrong.

This second type of paranoia marks a special stage of denial. In order to justify behavior that runs counter to that of their parents and friends, paranoid users believe that those others are out of touch with reality and with what should be important in their lives. This is another instance of drugs stunting emotional maturity so that the "I" is all-important.

Refusing at all costs to confront themselves with the facts of their behavior, these users focus the stress and anger this generates on everyone around them. In order to shift attention from their own failings, they'll expose others' faults. Parents can expect family battles, as these users will gleefully pounce on any parental shortcomings. Paranoiac users justify their behavior by feeling that they are being singled out for actions that others are getting away with or that parents and teachers are asking more of them than they do of siblings or other students. Not being liked and appreciated by these authority figures makes their lives a special trial, something to be relieved by—what else—more drugs.

Recklessness

Becomes increasingly adventuresome and thrill seeking
Growing impulsiveness
Increasingly exaggerated feelings of self-confidence
Places self in dangerous situations
Becomes accident prone

Reckless kids have an almost mystical belief that they are different and exempt from harm. They feel they can walk that thin line and not be consumed by the dangers on either side. Continued alcohol and other drug use only increases this false confidence, turning reckless kids into thrill seekers and odds defiers. While evident in all aspects of their lives, this is most appallingly obvious in their attitude toward driving: Kids on drugs too often believe beyond question that they can handle curves faster, beat trains at crossings, drink and drive. Parents will see the results in the form of traffic citations, minor crashes, arrests and, if the worst occurs, major crashes. Similar patterns apply to drug users' personal health: first occasional and then frequent minor scrapes and accidents and, in many cases, major injuries.

Acting on pure impulse, reckless kids seldom plan activities. In place of whatever others had planned they'll instigate an activity with an edge: joyriding, drinking and driving, vandalism. Organization disappears in their lives, replaced by a need for immediate gratification and risk.

Steroid users are especially prone to this behavior, an aspect of "roid rage." Use of steriods can make people short-tempered, abusive, adventuresome and definite thrill seekers. In their rage they'll take on the world and often push themselves beyond their limits. They assume larger-than-life, movie star personas, feeling that they can never be hurt, caught, injured or killed. Just the opposite is true. With bodies pushed physically to the limit, injuries are more frequent and take longer to heal. Steroid-induced rage creates a sense of arrogance, aggression and invincibility along with other psychological difficulties.

Hostility/Violence to Others

Becomes disobedient and rebellious to parents
Increasingly defiant of rules and regulations in general
Increasingly violent and threatening
Becomes verbally or physically abusive
Destroys or damages property in anger
Inflicts pain on self (cuts on arms, pokes with needles, etc.)

Recklessness and paranoia are a combination foredoomed to end in violence. When the natural rebelliousness felt by most youth is added to this combination, it becomes inevitable that parents will be the targets for much of this rage. (Though, as bar fights, brawls at sporting events and violence at parties prove, alcohol and other drugs will fuel violence wherever they are used.)

As authority figures, parents have the role of setting limits on their kids' behaviors, even those using drugs. Driven to attack those who have the power both to keep them from drugs and to force them to confront behavior that they know to be wrong, users will often lash out at their parents, siblings or other family members, either verbally or physically. Frustrated and angry, parents are likely to attack in kind, setting the stage for many nasty battles. These family wars can become extremely dangerous if the child is in a stage of rage from using steroids or if strung out on PCP.

Oddly, when they come down from their drug high hours later or the next day, users may well be apologetic for their behavior. Often they'll try to hide their behavior from the rest of their family, pleading with a sibling or one parent not to tell on them. In the depression that comes after much drug use (cocaine users are especially prone to depression after a high), low self-esteem users may hurt themselves as a means of punishment.

Violence can be spread over a continuum of behavior. Parents of late-stage drug abusers will likely see extremes of violence that they would otherwise not expect from their child. High levels of violence indicate that professional help is definitely needed.

Suicide

Suicidal children are ready to give up on life, and the drugs have only deepened their negative attitudes about themselves and the world. They believe there is little hope; they don't see much reason to live. Attempts at suicide may be a last ditch cry for help; although not every suicidal child does so, many will have given some earlier warning of suicide that was ignored, misinterpreted or not taken seriously, so that the actual attempt is made as an unmistakable way of calling attention to his or her plight. One study found that attempts at suicide outnumbered completed suicides by 100 to 1, with the attempts being grossly underreported even so. Every effort should be made to treat attempts or threats of suicide very seriously; those who attempt suicide are more likely to actually complete the act sometime in their future.

Children at risk for a suicide attempt have a remarkably similar profile to those who are at risk for drug problems. Suicidal children tend to feel low self-esteem, loneliness, hopelessness and a sense of feeling different, all made worse by depression.

Talking or writing about death or collecting potentially dangerous items such as razor blades, knives, firearms or pills are obvious warning signs for parents. More subtle indicators include the giving away of personal possessions; talk or writing about failure, worthlessness or isolation; breaking up with a boyfriend or girlfriend; and a sudden increase or decrease in eating or sleeping patterns. Attempted or completed suicides by friends or family members may trigger attempts by an at-risk youngster.

A number of studies have found that more children use drugs and poison in suicide attempts than any other method, another powerful reason to keep drugs out of the hands of children. In fact, drug availability seems to go hand in hand with suicide. When the number of barbiturate prescriptions written dropped by half from 1971 to 1976, so did the number of suicides attributable to barbiturates.

8

Red Flags: Changes in Activities and Habits

Parents may find it easier and less threatening to notice clues developing out of what their children do rather than who they are. Personality shifts tend to be subtle and subjective; changes in a child's appetite or in the condition of his or her room are not only more concrete but also don't reflect as badly on a parent as do lying and violence.

Parents needn't look for bizarre or exotic behavior to indicate drug use. Drugs tend to change the most basic daily activities—sleeping, eating, dressing, language—usually making them more erratic and swinging them further and further away from the behavior you had come to expect before your child started on drugs.

Insecure parents often undergo a battle between their suspicions and their trust for their children. Kids know this and understand that their parents are easy to manipulate, easy to con. Since there are only a few times in an average day at home that they have to be in a specified place at a specified time, youth can easily hide drug-induced behavior from parents who aren't alert. Parents who don't monitor their younger children's activities leave them unsupervised many hours a day, allowing time for kids to use drugs and to let drug effects slip away unrecognized.

Generally, kids can get away with much less of this in a structured situation outside the home. The odd behaviors created by drug use may be more easily noticeable in school or at work. For this reason, we've included sections on school- and work-related problems. Drugs crumble structure. If your child can't meet the normal demands of school or work, drugs may well be at fault.

Unexplained Absences

Increasingly often comes home late
Breaks curfew or sneaks out
Stays out later than before
Stays out overnight without telling you
Unable to account for time away from home
Withdraws into room for long periods
Sits in car alone
Frequently disappears for short periods of time
Volunteers to do chores that will require being out of parents' sight

Children on drugs are less inclined to lead normal lives. Parents of these kids often complain that the children they knew are no longer there. This is sometimes literally true. Parents genuinely see less of their children when they get involved with drugs. Three factors account for the various absences and disappearances users are prone to.

First, users will disappear so that they can get high in private. Kids who have a spot in the house to which they disappear for hours at a time may have created a drug haven. (See also Chapter 10, "Paraphernalia.") But absences don't have to be that long to be created by drugs. Many users will sneak away frequently for a quick toke on a joint or a visit to a hidden source of booze. Any excuse that takes them out of their parents' sight will be used. Kids on drugs will invent imaginary errands or seize upon real ones just to get out of the house. Those youth more heavily into drugs will be more blatant about their absences, spending as much time as possible off scoring—buying or otherwise obtaining drugs—and doing drugs and devoting a greater measure of their lives to their drug-using friends.

Second, drugs can alter users' perceptions of time. As we mentioned in the last chapter, as these kids become less aware of the passage of time they tend to be continually late for school, work or curfews. This lack of promptness doesn't bother them much. Not being able to admit to using drugs and no longer aware of or caring about the extent of their tardiness, users have absolutely no incentive to come up with satisfactory explanations for their lateness.

Third, parents should also be aware that as drugs cause users to withdraw more into themselves and create buffers against the non–drug-using world, users will develop a desire for more time alone, apart from their families. Odd excuses for their behavior will be made, such as wanting to spend an evening sitting in the family car in the driveway to "listen to music."

All absences are part of an overall breakdown in communication with parents and other family members. (See also Chapter 7, "Personality Shifts," "Parent/Family Relationships" and "Lateness.")

Household Responsibilities

No longer does chores: cutting grass, etc.
Forgets or refuses to participate in family occasions
Allows room to stay untidy
No longer organized and orderly

As kids on drugs withdraw from family life, their roles and responsibilities within the family become less important. Priorities set from the outside, especially by parents, fade in meaning. Chores seem irrelevant and trivial. Family functions are not only boring but may cut users off from their drug supplies by taking them out of their homes and away from their suppliers. Being asked to take care of younger sisters and brothers may be considered punishment because it means they can't leave the house to do drugs.

Other factors come into play as drug use increases. The drug user becomes increasingly unable to organize and plan and even simple chores become difficult. Many drugs interfere with short-term memory (see also Chapter 9, "Memory/Thought") so the user may honestly not remember a designated chore or family outing.

The more the child withdraws from family life, the more likely that drugs are playing their part.

Friendships/Communications

Makes frequent short trips with friends
Neglects to introduce friends to parents
Keeps friends from entering house when they call
Receives strange phone calls or calls at odd hours
Frequently borrows the car without explanation

New friends, changed relationships with old friends and friends hidden from parents: All are powerful clues to drug use.

Seeing friends is not by itself an indicator of drug use, but the making of frequent short trips may be, since the purpose for these trips is likely to be a quick high.

Frequent unexplained phone calls may mean that a child has become a drug supplier or at least one who shares alcohol or other drugs with his or her friends. The phone calls are intended to find out if, when and where the drug use or exchange will take place. If an adult answers the phone, the caller will often hang up. (See also Chapter 7, "Friends/Relationships.")

Friendships/Popularity

Gains sudden popularity
Displays sudden sexual activity
Becomes promiscuous
Acquires possessions from friends

Kids usually don't become popular overnight. Sudden popularity not only suggests the possibility that your child has become involved in drug use, but it is also a strong indicator that the child is a drug supplier or drug dealer. Small amounts of drugs, especially alcohol, may be obtainable at home or at parties, but larger and more regular supplies are going to be harder to come by. Kids also prefer scoring from someone their own age rather than from an adult dealer.

Kids with supplies of drugs can command others to come to them. Bold ones may even deal out of their own home. Wherever they go they'll be the center of attention, surrounded by drug users trying to make deals or just curry favor. Sometimes would-be purchasers will trade their possessions or steal goods from others to obtain drugs when they don't have the cash, so the sudden appearance of new clothes, CDs or cassettes, stereos or other luxuries in your home may indicate that your child has started to deal.

Sudden sexual activity or promiscuity suggests a drastic change in attitude and relationships, always indicators of possible drug use. Girls are particularly prone to offer sexual favors as a way of maintaining a "free" supply of drugs, although it is not uncommon for boys to do this as well. In the worst cases, addicted youths are persuaded to sell their bodies either for drug money or for the drugs themselves.

Eating Habits

Sudden increases in appetite
Sudden desire for sweets
Sudden loss of appetite
Develops general lack of interest in food and eating

In the sixties, movies about drugs almost always included a scene in which giggling pot smokers devoured huge quantities of pizza, chips, desserts and other snacks. The "munchies"—a sudden craving for food, especially sweets—are so notorious a product of smoking marijuana that the word became a basic part of drug lingo.

Today, other drugs are equally well known for their effect on appetites. Stimulants, especially amphetamines and their derivatives, are widely used as diet pills because they depress the appetite. Heavy cocaine users don't normally care much for food either, although a milder cocaine binge can sometimes stimulate tremendous hunger. Similarly, even though small amounts of alcohol are often consumed with food, heavy users of alcohol or other depressants often find that food is no longer greatly desired or appetizing.

Weight loss, which may be quite rapid, may be a result of drug use. Late-stage users are not able to physically camouflage the effects of their drug use. These users are totally preoccupied with getting high. Their weight loss is usually accompanied by other physical changes such as using less makeup, taking fewer baths and showers, pale complexion or messy hair. (See also Chapter 9, "Appearance/Hygiene.")

Sleeping-Pattern Change

Develops erratic sleeping patterns
Sleeps most of day but stays up nights

Most children establish a typical pattern of sleep. Drugs can throw these patterns out of whack either because the child is staying up late at night doing drugs or because the drugs themselves are overwhelming the body.

Stimulants may cause prolonged sleeplessness in the user; depressants and narcotics produce sedation and sleep. Users can no longer meet the normal schedule they once maintained.

When there is a sudden alteration in the hours that your children sleep or if their sleeping habits start to interfere on a regular basis with daily activities, such as school or work, you should suspect drug use.

Thievery/Hiding

Steals from house, car, school
Sells possessions
Constantly hides possessions
Caught hiding drugs, alcohol or cigarettes

Medicine or alcohol in home is missing
Lends possessions to friends
Claims money or possessions stolen

Drugs cost money, and regular drug use can cost a lot of money, especially for a child. Few children have the necessary funds to support their habits, and so they need access to drugs or money—both of which can be effortlessly found around their own homes.

While parents don't like to think about it, most homes are filled with drugs. Parents aren't likely to miss small amounts of booze taken from a bottle in the liquor cabinet or a few pills taken from a prescription. Paint thinner, glue and other inhalants can be stolen in great quantities before anyone would notice. Early-stage users don't need to pull more than an occasional theft. If you catch your children hiding alcohol or drugs, you should take it as a possible indication that they've moved to a later stage, in which their drug dependence is sufficiently serious that they must have access to an immediate supply of the drug to satisfy their cravings.

Money is the next target. Constant snitching of parents' bills and coins is bound to get noticed—even if only a few dollars are taken at any one time. After a while this small stuff may not satisfy larger habits or the desire to supply friends and get high outside of the home. Stashes of money are readily available within the home—from purses, wallets, pants pockets, dresser drawers and siblings' rooms. Thefts may start small but will increase with time. Personal items or seldom-used family possessions are another source of funds for drugs, since they can be sold or traded. Thefts of these items also take longer to be discovered.

Religion/Beliefs

Loses interest in church
Shows interest in occult or devil worship
Uncomfortable talking about religion or beliefs

Users' goals and values change under drugs. True, many teens set aside their religious upbringing. But a sudden desire not to attend church or church functions and a reluctance to talk about religion and beliefs on the part of a formerly religious youth is a strong indication of drug use. This may be part of the denial process, in which users can't reconcile what they know to be wrong behavior with the values they have been taught and so try to avoid confronting the representatives of those values.

Interest in the occult or devil worship may possibly indicate drug use. Devil worship makes very prominent use of alcohol and other drugs. Drugs are used in the occult to break down the participants' resistance and to magnify the unique experiences promised by those who control these activities. Interest in the occult does not necessarily mean participation, though: Many more of the trappings of devil worship exist than the actuality.

Language

Uses profanity excessively
Makes new friends who use bad language
Uses slang and drug terms you don't understand

Drug users like to think of themselves as different, special, a cut apart from the non–drug-using world. Drugs start this process; dress, appearance, friends, values and language continue it. Parents should remember this from the youth culture of the sixties, in which words like pot, toke, joint, trip, acid and stoned all formed part of a drug culture supposedly unintelligible to adults.

Employing language that parents do not understand or that is likely to shock them gives users a sense of self-importance. It also binds the user closer to others who share these alternative values and allows them to identify more closely with those who literally share the same language. Parents should make a special effort to learn their children's slang: If they don't understand the terms, how can they tell which are drug related?

Condition of Room

Bedroom is cold even in winter
Airs out room frequently
Uses fans at all times to circulate air
Uses incense, breath fresheners, room deodorizers, perfume, cologne
Keeps parents out of room
Keeps a locked box that no one else can open

Drug users will likely spend many of their waking hours in their bedrooms. This suits their increasing sense of isolation, gives them a territory that is theirs and away from their parents and provides them with a place in which to do drugs unobserved.

Many young users consider marijuana a popular drug to do in the bedroom, but the resulting smoke and strong odor make its use easy to detect. Users will open windows or use fans to blow out the smoke and burn incense to cover up the odor. A fan in the window in winter is a strong clue. Room deodorizers, cologne and other fresheners are commonly used to mask the scent of marijuana and other drugs in rooms or vehicles or on users' bodies.

Hiding drugs and drug paraphernalia is as much a necessity for users as hiding drugs' telltale residues. A perpetually locked door or a child nervous about having parents enter may well mean that that child is hiding drugs. More sophisticated users will allow parents in but will keep a lock box or similar personal storage device for drugs and paraphernalia. (See also Chapter 10, Paraphernalia.)

Overly Interested in Youth Music and Concerts

Let's make one thing clear: Rock music does not cause drug use, and neither does heavy metal, rap, punk, hip hop, thrash or any of the other variants of today's youth music. Instead, rock in all its many guises creates a youth culture, with its own language, styles, dress and experience, one designed to keep parents out.

Youth music appeals to all kids but is especially appealing to those who already believe that their drug use sets them apart from the non–drug-using world. These kids use their identification with music figures—many of whom are well known for their own drug use—to further distance themselves from their parents. Concerts, despite efforts to clean them up, are still notorious for drug use. Since the drugs are supposed to enhance the total sensory experience of the music, concerts, unless rigorously supervised, are considered ideal sites for kids to buy and get high on alcohol, pills, marijuana and hallucinogens.

Ironically, the number of overt drug references in youth music is probably less today than it was at the height of hippie culture in the 1960s, and more music-industry stars are ditching alcohol and other drugs and preaching the anti-drug message. Even so, the outlaw image generated by some musicians, especially those in heavy metal and rap, means that they will always have a large following among kids who see themselves as outlaws because of their own drug use.

School-Related Problems

Not doing homework
Drop in grades
Increasing neglect of school work
Decreasing motivation in school
Frequently late for school
Falls asleep in class
Skips classes or entire days
Develops sudden discipline problems
Frequently disciplined or suspended
Drops after-school activities
Hangs out with new group
Tries to get parents to take side against school representatives
Becomes disrespectful of teachers, rules and regulations
Drops out of school
Gets expelled from school

School Red Flags tend to mirror in more specific form the general ones we've been discussing in this and the last chapter. The causes of users' behavior are the same: lack of motivation, lack of interest, personality changes, new friends, physical problems caused by drugs. The Red Flags listed above run the gamut from those likely to be seen in earliest Stage 1 use to the total alienation found in Stage 3 or 4 users.

For most kids, school is their biggest single activity, using up the most hours and requiring the most attention, discipline and concentration. Little wonder that when drugs become a factor in their lives, the effects may well become noticeable in school even before parents are aware of them in the home. Parents may overlook neglected chores, but teachers will always comment on missed homework. Kids are free to wander in and out at home, where mealtimes may be flexible and adults preoccupied, but similar behavior in a classroom can be grounds for suspension. Parents need to pay special attention to reports of their children's behavior in schools: Teachers may be perceiving things that parents can't see.

Minor school problems will only get worse if alcohol and other drug use dominates the user's life. Incidents may start small—a slight drop in grades, less motivation for school work—but will build and multiply. The physical effects of drugs—mental slowness, befuddlement, disorientation, stupor—create the exact opposite of the mental state needed for learning.

Users won't accept the blame for their own actions: They'll complain that teachers' don't like them or that counselors and principals have it in for them. They'll ask parents to take their side, make excuses for tardiness or skipped classes and ignore suspensions or other punishments. As schoolwork slides, so will extracurricular activities no matter how desirable they once might have been.

Heavy drug users are such problem students that no schools will put up with them—and they probably won't put up with the schools. Drugs and dropouts are known to go together: Dropouts do more drugs than their counterparts who stay in school.

Job-Related Problems

Increasingly uses sick time on job
Increasing number of on-the-job accidents
More frequently late for work
Develops sudden increased popularity with co-workers
Displays sudden worsening of relations with co-workers
Shows increasing disrespect for supervisors, rules, and regulations
Spends too much time smoking cigarettes
Leaves work area frequently
Goes to out-of-the-way locations during breaks
Regularly visits areas without legitimate reason for doing so
Regularly has visits by strangers
Regularly has visits by other employees with no legitimate reason in that work area
Receives secretive phone calls

Many factors—the growth of the fast-food and service economies, which need huge numbers of workers; the expensive shoes and flashy clothes that teens long for; the economic stagnation that has kept parents' real incomes from expanding for a decade—have created a world in which teenagers are again near their post–World War II peak in percentage of employment. States are even passing laws to keep teens from working "part-time" jobs for more hours than most full-time adults do. Huge numbers of dropouts are also on the streets looking for full-time jobs to support themselves—and, in many cases, to support spouses and children.

The same lack of self-discipline and physical disorientation that causes problems in schools will create even more noticeable ones on the job.

Tardiness at school translates to being late for work; skipped classes to missed days of work or increased sick days; talking back to teachers to disrespect for supervisors. Worse, workplaces are usually more dangerous than schools, and so drugs and alcohol play an enormous role in on-the-job accidents.

Workplaces—where everyone is likely to have money—also make drug dealing easier. Employers who know of employees who are suddenly popular with co-workers, have regular visits by strangers or visit co-workers without a legitimate reason for being in that work area can often legitimately suspect that drug dealing or supplying is taking place.

It's harder for parents to see the effects of drugs on their children's jobs than it is in the home. Still, parents should be alert to their children taking large numbers of sick days, being hurt frequently on the job or showing a pattern of job turnover, whether from frequently quitting or getting fired. And, of course, many parents are employers of their own or other people's children and need to be alert to the harm that drug users can do to themselves and to their jobs if they get high at work.

9

Red Flags: Changes in
Physical Appearance

Drug highs come from inside the body as drugs work on brains, nervous systems and metabolisms. Nevertheless, drugs are so potent that their effects are often visible from the outside.

We talk far more about individual drugs in this chapter than in other Red Flag chapters because each specific drug leaves characteristic markings on the body, easily visible to those who know what to look for. They way a drug is used—smoked, inhaled, injected—will also be apparent. Even when users try to cover up their drug use, these Red Flags will be apparent.

Parents also need to watch out for more general effects of drugs. Kids who use drugs heavily are simply not going to be as healthy or as physically well developed as those who don't. Just as drugs stunt emotional growth, drug abuse, especially by younger kids, will stunt physical growth. Prepubescent alcoholics and addicts jeopardize their entire future. (Steroids are an exception here—some users will appear abnormally well developed, although their long-term health will still be affected.)

Drugs are potent chemicals. It's been said that there are no such things as side effects to drugs: Every consequence is an effect; some are simply unwanted. Drug use inevitably brings about these unwanted effects. Physical side effects are tremendously useful to parents as Red Flags warning of their children's drug use.

Health

Weight loss
Colds, flu, stomach cramps or aches, fatigue
Chronic cough
Chest pains
Frequent illness
Hangovers
Sick in the morning, okay by noon
Frequently injured from falls or fights
More frequent sports injuries with slow recovery

The use of alcohol and other drugs puts a strain on the body. Drug highs come specifically from the way stimulants, depressants and narcotics alter the internal body functions of those who consume them. No one should expect to ravage their bodies with potent chemicals without a price, and the price is high—even ignoring the cancers, liver and kidney failures and heart and lung diseases that are possible long-term consequences of heavy drug use.

Each and every time users think they are enjoying drugs, their bodies must waste energy countering their effects. Bodies want to run at a nice stable equilibrium, an even keel destroyed by drugs spiraling systems out of control. Users' own bodies start fighting drugs immediately, trying to keep their internal systems at close-to-normal levels, while at the same time processing and filtering the drugs out of the bloodstream. Users can spare little energy for maintaining a strong immune system to combat the everyday ills that most of us can avoid or shrug off without effect.

Users might have more success in throwing off the effects of their drug use if they stayed in peak condition. Few do. Most regular users spend little time exercising or working out to stay healthy, leading to overall loss of muscle tone and fitness. They are also prone to bumps and bruises from the minor accidents, vehicle and otherwise, they tend to incur.

Certain drugs actually attack the body's defenses, as cocaine does when it destroys the hairs in the nose instrumental in filtering out airborne cold germs. Other drugs create their own ailments: Tobacco and marijuana can lead to chronic coughing, stimulants can cause chest pains, alcohol can cause headaches and hangovers. Many drugs and combinations of drugs depress appetite and cause major weight loss: This is the actual function of the stimulant-based diet pills. (See also Chapter 8, "Eating Habits.")

Young steroid users can show phenomenal muscle growth in weeks, but this growth, combined with the heavy physical activity the growth is intended to accompany, puts a heavy strain on tendons and ligaments. Steroid use eventually results in more frequent injuries, more severe injuries and slower recovery rates. Steroids are also now known to disrupt the body's immune system.

Physical Development

Exhibits disrupted growth patterns
Shows sudden tremendous muscular development
Has little energy
Loses sexual interest
Bulimia
Irregular menstruation

If kids thought rationally, they would realize that there are few worse times in life than adolescence to be saturating their bodies with drugs. Growth and physical development are an essential part of growing up. Using drugs as a preteenager can slow and stunt this development. Those foolish enough to get into drugs before puberty can leave their bodies years behind those of non–drug users.

The high metabolic rate and consequent tremendous appetites of teen-agers often fall victim to drugs. A significant percentage of bulimics use such drugs as alcohol and amphetamines and also use more marijuana, cocaine and barbiturates than those without this eating disorder. Heavy depressant use also succeeds in killing appetites because the depressants function by slowing body functions. Alcohol by itself contains large num-bers of calories—but virtually no nutritional value. Kids getting an over-abundance of calories from alcohol are probably too bloated to each much else and are surely not eating a balanced diet. (See also Chapter 8, "Eating Habits.")

The chemicals in steroids are deliberately chosen to mimic those that cause the enormous muscular growth associated with puberty. Sudden physical development—accompanied by a 15- to 20-pound weight gain in one to two months—by teenage athletes should be suspect. Steroid use in girls, while still rare, leads to disrupted menstrual cycles and the develop-ment of "masculine" characteristics—increased facial hair, permanent deepening of the voice.

Overuse of many drugs, individually or especially in combination, will lead to impotence in males and a general loss of interest in sex.

Speech

Becomes incoherent
Slurred speech
Rapid speech with no slowdown
Speaks with jumbled words

Users can never limit drugs' effects just to the highs they crave. Drugs always spread their webs over every part of the body. Take alcohol as an example. Alcohol is a depressant, and that means its use slows bodily functions and destroys the fine control needed to make the body work. Those high on alcohol find it harder to come up with words and harder still to make their mouths say them properly, creating the well-known slurred speech of the drunk. Other depressants, such as the barbiturates and sedatives, will cause similar speech slurring—but so will LSD, PCP and similar drugs.

Cocaine and other stimulants have an opposite effect, resulting in rapid and constant speech. Fast-talking jumbles of words known as "speed raps" are a hallmark of the amphetamine user.

Indeed, speech is such a complex act requiring so much brain and muscular coordination that the use of almost any drug will quickly produce an effect: PCP, repetitive speech; inhalants, jumbled words; LSD and PCP, among many drugs, incoherence.

Although a few diseases produce bizarre speech behavior, drug-induced speech problems should be differentiable from most long-term developmental difficulties by their sudden onset and their disappearance after the drug has worn off. Whenever a child suddenly has difficulty in speaking or is mumbling or talking wildly and incoherently, drugs should be suspected.

Memory/Thought

Experiences blackouts
Suffers from memory loss
Experiences hallucinations or flashbacks
Suffers from muddled thinking

Drugs can interfere with memory and mental alertness: Regular drug users do not have the same daily thought processes they did before the start of the drug use. Some of these changes are short-term, some of them long.

Even in the absence of other physical signs, parents should be able to observe that children coming home drunk or stoned are less sharp and aware than before they left. Most adults are familiar with the way alcohol muddles thinking. Marijuana affects short-term memory, noticeable in gaps in speech, groping for words and in increased danger while driving. Stimulants distort thinking, often leaving users with an air of arrogance or paranoia; depressants impair and slow down thought; PCP can make users believe themselves to be invincible.

Teachers often note these changes before parents do: Kids who show up at school high on drugs will learn less and at a slower rate, forget assignments, flunk tests and may wind up being held back or dropping out of school. (See also Chapter 8, "School-Related Problems.")

A word about blackouts: Blackouts are not the equivalent of passing out, even though drugs will make some users pass out as well. In a true blackout, users are conscious but will later remember nothing of what they said or did and may deny their actions even if told to them by witnesses. Most blackouts are rather brief, lasting anywhere from a few moments to an evening, but long-term alcoholics can experience blackouts lasting for weeks or months.

The hallucinogens will bring about conscious hallucinations both shortly after the drug is taken and again—sometimes repeatedly—days, months or years later, at which point they are called flashbacks.

Eyes

Bloodshot, puffy or glassy eyes
Dilated or constricted pupils
Droopy eyelids or sleepy appearance
Lack of control of eye movements
Blurred or double vision
Irritated eyes

Eyes are a great giveaway of drug use: Virtually all drugs create effects that show up in and around the eyes.

The puffy, bloodshot eyes of the alcoholic are well known. Puffy eyes along with a flushed face are signs of inhalant use. Barbiturates and PCP can produce blurred or double vision. Stimulant users may have difficulty in focusing. Those on an LSD trip can be found with a blank, fixed stare as they watch things nobody else can see.

The bloodshot eyes of marijuana users are so notorious that they are a standard joke in the drug culture. Heavy users may wear sunglasses constantly, although this is hardly a sign of marijuana use alone. Sunglasses worn inside may indicate the use of any of several categories of drugs. Cocaine, other stimulants, amphetamines and LSD all dilate the pupils, making them highly sensitive to light. Inhalants irritate the eyes so badly that sunglasses may be necessary. Constricted pupils, on the other hand, are a sign of both narcotics and PCP, which also gives the eyelids a droopy effect.

PCP, LSD, alcohol and other depressants and inhalants can produce a condition known as "gaze nystagmus," in which users cannot keep their pupils still; their eyes move involuntarily.

Nose

Sensitive or runny nose
Sores around nostrils
Sneezing
Nosebleeds

The nose is a sensitive and delicate organ. The hairs and membranes lining the inner passages of our nostrils are easily damaged. Any drug that is snorted or inhaled can destroy these tissues.

Kids who use inhalants may show signs of a runny nose, nosebleeds and sneezing, as will those who are on narcotics. Cocaine is extremely damaging to the nose and users are prone to all the Red Flags listed above. In fact, one of the many reasons snorting cocaine is on its way out is because users have stopped being willing to put up with the way cocaine irritates their nostrils or even literally destroys the tissues inside.

Mouth

Dry mouth
Frequently licks lips with tongue
Breath smells of alcohol/marijuana/tobacco
Coughing

Just as inhaling a drug irritates the nose, smoking irritates the mouth and lungs. Many drugs create symptoms that show in the mouth. You'd expect smokers of marijuana and tobacco to cough a lot, but coughing is also a sign of inhalant use. Smoke will create dry mouths, but so will barbiturates, amphetamines and LSD.

Both the smoke from marijuana and tobacco and the flavorings in most alcoholic beverages leave odors that are easily detectable during speech or a kiss, forcing users to try to cover them up. Smoking marijuana, which often involves getting the last pieces of the drug out of the hot butt of a joint, is also known for the chapped lips that its users develop, forcing them to lick their lips regularly or use commercial lip balm.

Skin

Injection marks along veins
Wears long-sleeve or high-collar shirts, even on warmer days
Mutilates self (tattoos or burn marks)
Discolored fingers
Excessive perspiration
Cold and clammy skin
Itching and burning skin
Sudden acne
Tight, swollen or puffy skin
Jaundice (a condition characterized by yellowness of skin and whites of eyes)
Purple or red spots on the body
Unexplained darkening of the skin

As recently as a few years ago, few kids injected their drugs, for several good reasons. Injections were mainly for drugs like heroin that even users thought dangerous. They also required hard-to-get needles, caused pain, created more powerful rushes but quicker addictions and left noticeable marks behind.

Today the needle has become popular because of the quickly spreading use of steroids. Steroid users poke their needles into muscles rather than veins as hard-core heroin addicts do, but either way, visible signs of use—needle marks, injection sores, itching and burning skin, collapsed veins—or attempts to cover them are sure indicators of heavy drug use.

Although the use of needles is most likely a sign of steroid use today, many other drugs can come in injectable form and are most dangerous this way.

Needle tracks are a hallmark of the heroin addict. Most addicts inject into their arms, but those trying to hide their habits may inject into their legs instead. Heavy use makes veins collapse, and so addicts will then inject the drug into other areas of the body, anywhere they can find veins still in good shape.

Steroid users don't inject as regularly as heroin addicts, though during a steroid "cycle"—a period of several weeks of using the drug, followed by an equivalent period off—they will inject frequently. They also prefer "butt hits," injections to the upper rear buttock, the most heavily muscled area of the body. These needle marks are well hidden from exposure and do not show as conspicuously as marks in the more tender skin on the forearm.

Steroids, drugs that are designed to produce changes in the body, affect skin as well as muscles. Severe acne is often a side effect of steroid use. Users are also likely to develop pink and puffy skin and a swollen face and neck and to have their skin stretched tight over newly formed muscles. Skin color can be affected either by jaundice turning skin yellow or a darkening of the skin.

Other drugs show up on the skin in different ways. Smoking either tobacco or marijuana can discolor fingers. Alcohol often leaves the skin feeling cold and clammy. Many drugs cause their users to sweat profusely: amphetamines, LSD, even cocaine, which can produce high body temperatures in large doses.

Motor Control

Loss of motor control
Becomes jittery or overactive
Slow gait
Poor balance
Clumsiness
Dizziness
Muscle fatigue

Depressants can slow body functions, and the fine control needed to move our bodies is one of the first functions affected. The shuffling gait of the drunk is familiar to most people, and sedatives, barbiturates and tranquilizers in large doses will produce similar clumsiness. Any task involving fine muscular control will be made more difficult. Even many mild over-the-counter medications from the depressant family come with a warning that users should not drive or operate heavy machinery under their influence.

Loss of motor control is not limited to the depressants, however. Large amounts of almost any drug will keep the user from moving normally. Cocaine users find their bodies racing so much that they have great difficulty in keeping still. Inhalants destroy balance and coordination. LSD has recently been found to cause "freezing" or "jamming," during which users' muscles lock on them, leaving the victims conscious but unable to move for minutes, hours or longer.

Few drug users recognize how badly their motor control has been affected by the drugs. They'll insist that they are fine and that their walk, as well as their speech or motor control, is perfectly normal. Far too many automobile crashes stem from this denial of reality.

Appearance/Hygiene

Flaunts new hair or clothing styles
Displays drug-oriented graffiti, decals, t-shirts, etc.
Shows changes in personal hygiene
Develops permanently slovenly appearance

Simply using drugs is not sufficient for many youth. They'll adopt any apparel or attire they can find that screams to the non–drug-using world how different they are, how far apart from the non–drug users they've grown. Although kids are always eager to sport the latest fads, the sudden appearance of drug-oriented material is a very strong indicator of drug approval. This material may take a number of forms: graffiti on book covers, art class projects, bumper stickers, decals, shirts and hats with drug or alcohol themes, drug-oriented magazines or books.

Drug-oriented jewelry is also popular among users. This may take the form of spoons, gold straws or medallions with marijuana leaves hung from neck chains, marijuana leaf rings, small pipes clipped to clothing or any of a variety of objects that symbolize drugs.

Hair styles, clothing and accessories may change as the user begins to conform to the dress of the local drug world, although parents are more likely just to be aware of the newness and strangeness of these styles than their specific drug meanings. Still, if the drug themes become blatant, parents should not be conned by children trying to justify this behavior as a fad or something that all the other kids are doing. Kids are the last to wear anything that they dislike or don't believe in. If they're wearing drug-oriented clothing, they're doing so out of approval for drugs.

Early-stage users may use dressing up as a way to show their allegiance to their newfound friends, but this will change as the user progresses further and further into drug use. Lack of normal hygiene and cleanliness is not related to the familiar sloppy appearance of youth but are pathological life-style alterations. A permanently slovenly teenager may be passing from Stage 2 to Stage 3 use. These later-stage users no longer care much about clothes, appearance or even cleanliness and basic hygiene. Users may not bother to wash themselves, their hair or their clothes. Their rooms or homes will become equally dirty. When living on their own, food may be eaten off dirty dishes and cooked in filthy pots.

Part of this degradation of the self stems from the low self- esteem that heavy drug users often suffer from (see also Chapter 7, "Low Self-esteem") and part from the fact that in these late stages drugs so dominate the users' lives that grooming becomes entirely secondary to the constant search to obtain drugs and get high.

10

Red Flags: Paraphernalia

Most Red Flags are warnings, not proof, of drug use. For three chapters we've described signs that taken together would be a completely damning picture of a child on drugs but individually could easily be explained away. Sometimes parents are right to dismiss thoughts of drug use; sometimes they are simply practicing denial. With paraphernalia we come to the realm of hard evidence.

We urge all parents to take a trip to their local head shop or smoke shop—stores that sell products that are technically licit but obviously intended for drug use—to see for themselves the tremendous variety of objects for sale. As parents you need to see the real things with your own eyes so that you will be able to recognize them when they appear in your child's bedroom. Your kids are counting on your ignorance to save them from the consequences of their behavior.

Drugs are potent, so normally only small amounts of them are needed. These small amounts can, with a little ingenuity, be stashed in almost any conceivable hiding place. Unless parents are willing to open their minds to the possibility that drugs can be kept literally anywhere, they will miss some of the most damning clues to their children's drug use.

Pipes

Pipes vary from ordinary store-bought tobacco pipes made out of wood, to giant foot-high or larger glass contraptions called "bongs" or "bhongs," to metal hookahs. Many are tiny metal or glass pipes just a few inches long, whose bowls are much too small to hold a sufficient amount of tobacco.

These pipes can, however, hold enough hashish to get someone high. Some of the largest pipes are so elaborate and showy that users will often claim that they are only for display. Rarely will this be true. Most probably, any variety of pipe has only one real purpose—heating and inhaling drugs.

Users who can't buy pipes or don't want to leave them around to cause suspicion can easily make their own. One ingenious home-made pipe involves nothing more than an ordinary pop can. Kids dent the sides of the can and punch several holes in the dented area. After they fill the depression made by the dent with marijuana and light it, the marijuana smoke can be sucked out of the can's normal opening. Once the drug is smoked, all that is left is a crumpled can that no one would suspect had any connection with drugs. A plain toilet paper roll can be turned into a smoking tool by punching holes in it large enough to fit the end of a marijuana joint. With their lips on one end sucking in the smoke and their hand over the other hand to hold the smoke in, kids have just created a disposable homemade pipe that allows them to pull in more smoke with each puff than is possible with a joint alone. Even a rolled-up piece of aluminum foil can be used for smoking pot. Kids are endlessly creative in thinking up new ways to use drugs.

Pipe Accessories

Small, round pieces of screen about the size of a dime are used for filtering substances when they are heated and smoked in a pipe. An even more common accessory are pipe cleaners—long, thin pieces of soft material wrapped around wires, about four to six inches long, used to clean pipes. Anyone who uses a pipe or smokes regularly will need matches or lighters. Lighters are often prized possessions, gold plated or with the users' initials. They may even come shaped as other objects, such as small guns. Since they seem innocuous, these accessories are often left out in the open.

Rolling Papers

Back in 1972, a man named Burt Rubin grew frustrated when he found that he constantly needed two sheets of standard tobacco rolling paper to make a full joint. He produced a bigger sheet called EZ Wider. In a few years he had a multi- million-dollar business. He's since been copied by others, and all of their products are available at paraphernalia shops and even many

drugstores. Although a few adults may still roll their own tobacco cigarettes, rolling papers are a sure sign of marijuana use by youth. Users
will even leave the papers in the open, banking on their parents' ignorance to save them from punishment. Tim remembers one particular
child well:

> A *mother called me one day to ask if rolling papers could be used to clean glasses
> as her son had told her. I asked her to bring the boy in. First thing, I told him that
> I had 12 years on the police department with the last five in narcotics. Instantly,
> sweat rolled down the kid's forehead. I showed him the ridges on the papers and
> explained that I knew the ridges were for holding the marijuana on the paper. He
> started to cry, admitting that he had lied and got high every day before school. We
> got him help and to this day he is still clean.*

Containers for Storing Substances

Kids know that parents may not be suspicious all the time but that they'll
pounce on anything that looks like a drug or an obvious drug accessory.
Drugs have to be hidden. This is a game of wits between parents and
children that the children can easily win. Except for some of the largest and
showiest pipes and bhongs, what they have to hide is small and, for the
most part, flexible enough to be jammed into tight spaces.

Users know that their parents are looking for the unusual, so pipes and
the drugs themselves are likely to be stored in the most common, everyday
items users can find. These include popular small, yellow coin envelopes
and other clear plastic envelopes, plastic bags of different sizes and a
variety of other containers: makeup kits, plastic film containers, cigarette
packs, bottles, small glass vials and cans.

Fake cans and other look-alikes are sold in paraphernalia shops and are
even available in catalogs. These cans have false bottoms or tops that screw
out to reveal a hollow compartment in which to store drugs. Fakes are made
of every conceivable can sold in the United States. Some of these fakes
have an upper portion that actually works, dispensing spray deodorant or
other innocuous products. Fakes are not sold as drug containers, of course;
often they are advertised as having legitimate uses such as hiding away
money or jewelry.

Parents should also watch for items that appear and disappear. Users
hide full containers but leave empty ones out to divert suspicion, training
parents to get used to seeing these objects. On weekends or when drug
parties are planned, these containers will suddenly vanish.

Clips

Marijuana is more expensive than cigarettes. Users don't like to waste the butts and so will try to smoke a joint until it disappears. To keep from burning their fingers on the last few puffs, they'll hold it with some sort of clip. Bent paper clips will do in a pinch, as will the alligator clips used in making electrical connections. Paraphernalia shops sell special "roach" clips similar in appearance, so-called because the end of a joint is called a roach. Fake keys are made that separate like a small scissors so they can be used as roach clips: These are easily concealed on a key ring. Medical-style hemostats are frequently used for this purpose by those who can get their hands on them.

Rags or Bags with Traces of Chemicals on Them

The fumes from inhalants—glue, solvents and other chemicals or household products that kids sniff to get high—are most potent when concentrated. Users often pour or spray inhalant liquids onto rags or into paper and plastic bags or other containers to make it easier for them to bring the concentrated fumes right up to their nose. Parents may find these chemical-soaked bags in wastepaper baskets or as part of a room's general litter. Often the smell of the chemicals lingering on the bags will alert parents. Parents may also suspect the use of these chemicals by smelling the countermeasures—incense, room deodorizer, perfume or cologne—used to hide the odors. (See also Chapter 8, "Condition of Room.")

Needles

Any time a child has legitimate reasons for possessing hypodermic needles—diabetes, for example—parents will know about it. Otherwise, your discovery of a needle can indicate only one thing: Your child is using dangerous drugs.

Youngsters involved with muscle sports—football, weightlifting, bodybuilding—may feel pressure to inject themselves with steroids, although steroid use has recently expanded to youngsters who merely wish to improve their appearance. Narcotics and other drugs are also injected by some users because they get a more immediate and more powerful rush that way.

Not only is using a needle dangerous (see also Chapter 9, "Skin"), but sharing needles has been known to cause high school steroid users to spread the AIDS virus as well. Heroin users are even more notoriously connected with spreading AIDS.

Over-the-Counter Medications and Products

Sunglasses
Eyedrops
Nasal spray
Lip moisturizers
Cough drops or lozenges
Aspirin, acetaminophen, ibuprofen

As we noted in Chapter 9, drugs will produce a variety of uncomfortable and noticeable effects on the body. Kids will try to hide these from their parents. Sunglasses will be worn, even inside, to conceal the effect of marijuana, alcohol, inhalants and cocaine, among other drugs, on their eyes. Eyedrops will be employed to banish the redness from bloodshot eyes and the discomfort produced by alcohol or marijuana.

Cocaine severely irritates nasal passages. So many of the fine hairs on the nose are destroyed that nasal spray is necessary to help heavy users breathe. Tobacco or marijuana smoke gives most users a cough, dry mouth and chapped lips, requiring a bevy of medications to counteract these symptoms.

Alcohol hangovers are probably the most common drug symptom of all, and any number of hangover cures will be tried, including plain old aspirin or other pain relievers like acetaminophen and ibuprofen.

Although not drug accessories in the traditional sense, these items are listed here as reminders to start looking at the entire spectrum of your children's behaviors for anything out of the ordinary, any changes in their habits, anything they may be trying to hide from you, any objects you don't understand and they are unwilling to explain. Drugs will infiltrate every aspect of your children's lives. As parents you must be willing to follow.

11

Red Flags: Legal Problems

Marijuana, cocaine, LSD, PCP and other popular drugs are controlled substances. Although penalties vary from state to state, often depending on the amount found, both possession and sale are illegal throughout the country. For those under the legal age—usually 21 for alcohol and 18 to tobacco—purchasing these products is similarly illegal, even if seldom enforced.

While charges of drug possession may be parents' nightmares, drugs will lead children into many more types of problems with authorities. The ever-present need to obtain quantities of drugs and the irresponsibility and loss of control from being on drugs together generate much of the crime, both simple thefts and violent crime, in this country. Drug- and alcohol-related automobile and other vehicle crashes kill tens of thousands and injure hundreds of thousands more each year. Drug-induced hostility to any figures of authority brings about many more problems that, while not technically illegal, greatly affect users' lives.

This is a short chapter only because the categories tend to be so all-encompassing. Drugs create the problems that are destroying so many of our cities and so many of the youth within. Parents whose kids are on drugs should expect to become very familiar with the legal system.

Automobile

Involved in auto accidents or near misses
Receives excessive traffic citations
Arrested for DUI or DWI

Drinking and driving don't mix. That's a message we've all heard over the years. Less publicized are the number of crashes and citations brought about because of the use of other drugs. It's likely that these are underreported because alcohol is often consumed together with these drugs and it is easier to test for alcohol intake than for anything else.

No matter what the drug is or the quantity used—a single drink or marijuana cigarette can impair reflexes sufficiently to cause a crash—drug users don't belong behind the wheel of a car, truck, motorcycle, snowmobile, boat or any other vehicle. A pattern of citations, crashes or even bumps and dents in the car (often unreported to the insurance company) is a strong clue to drug use.

Charged with Crime

Charged with theft
Caught shoplifting
Charged with prostitution
Charged with breaking and entering or burglary
Charged with possession or drug dealing

Crimes tend to increase in number and seriousness as drug use increases. Shoplifting, for example, implies a regular user who needs possessions to barter for drugs, but breaking and entering probably implies a more severe habit and greater need for drug money. Girls who trade favors for drugs may turn to prostitution to maintain a regular supply as their habit intensifies.

Serious users know that what they are doing is wrong, but the combination of their lack of money and need for drugs drives them into crime, often to be caught along with friends in similar need. When youth are caught with or have stolen large amounts of money or drugs, dealing is almost certainly involved.

Violent Crimes

Caught vandalizing or damaging property
Charged with assault or related charges
Charged with violent crimes
Possesses guns or other weapons

The recklessness and violence that are so closely associated with drugs (see also Chapter 7, "Recklessness" and "Hostility/Violence to Others") will eventually involve others.

Property damage may come first: Kids on drugs have been known to vandalize homes, schools, cemeteries and signs and symbols of authority. This behavior is especially common when gangs of kids—their judgment and responsibility destroyed by drugs—egg each other on.

For many, the next step involves physical assaults. Many of them are gang- or group-related assaults. Many colleges, for example, are restricting alcohol at fraternities and other student organizations because a frightening number of assaults and sexual assaults are being reported.

Individual users are also prone to physical violence. Assaults are a serious indication of lack of control from drugs or their heavy use. The Department of Justice has estimated that more than 80% of criminals arrested for violent felonies were on drugs when they committed their crimes. Once violent behavior starts, it will likely happen again. Parents need to be cautious in dealing with a violent drug user in their home. Parents are tempting targets for violence both because they are close at hand and because they often try to keep the user from drugs and the drug scene.

12

How to Help

Now is the time to talk to your children about drugs.

Now is always the right time, no matter what age your children are and whether or not you've found Red Flags that apply to them. Just as parents start talking about sex at an early age, making their information more explicit and detailed as children grow older, you need to start hammering home the message that drugs are wrong as early as possible, changing only the specifics as your children grow. If you haven't already done so, do it now. It is never too early and never too late to talk to your children about drugs.

When you do talk to your children, you need to keep in mind their probable drug experience. Use our chapters on Red Flags as guidance. Place your children into one of three possible categories:

1. **No visible Red Flags.** Consider yourself fortunate, but remain open to the consideration that there might be a possibility of a drug problem. Although your children may never have tried drugs or may have experimented with them and given them up, the odds are that they are using alcohol or other drugs but in too small quantities or too infrequently for you to notice the signs.

   Remember that virtually all kids try drugs by the time they leave high school and that most start much earlier. Reported use of the gateway drugs—marijuana as well as alcohol and cigarettes—remains high all the way through school. Parents need to reinforce the standard that no drug use is acceptable, and they have to try to educate their children that even the occasional use of drugs is risky. Surprisingly few youth already believe this. Kids can easily go from the very occasional use of drugs to a dangerous binge without realizing what they're getting themselves into.

2. A *few visible* Red Flags. Many parents, especially as their children grow older, will notice Red Flags in their kids' behaviors. Over one-third of high school seniors admit to having had five or more drinks in a row sometime in the past two weeks. Nearly one in five smokes cigarettes daily. Close to a quarter have used illicit drugs within the past month. This level of drug use will betray obvious Red Flags that you should now be able to recognize. When you start seeing Red Flags in your children, it's time to confront them with your evidence and work with them to put an end to their drug use.

3. *Many obvious* Red Flags. A small percentage of parents, whether because of their ignorance of drugs or sheer denial, will now be forced to admit for the first time that one or more of their children uses drugs regularly or binges heavily. Confrontation with the user is now inevitable, and the probability of putting that child in a treatment program looms.

Perhaps surprisingly, there are many more similarities than differences in how parents should approach their children with a discussion of drugs and drug use, no matter how many Red Flags are showing. We'll detail what those steps should be and what to do when more urgent measures are required. But first, parents need to look at themselves and their attitudes toward drugs. Kids will detect the slightest hypocrisy in their parents' words. If you want what you say about drugs to be effective, be sure that your actions match your words.

Parents' Attitudes Toward Drugs

Our kids did not invent drugs or drug use. They learned it from us. Adults push drugs on youth in a thousand ways—on the streets, yes, but also in television beer commercials, magazine cigarette ads, glamorous portrayals of drug users in movies and in parents' behavior at home.

Before launching an attack on your kids for their use of drugs, think carefully about the way drugs are used in your own home.

▼　How do you relax after a hard day at work? If it's by stopping off at a bar for a few beers or pouring yourself a drink as soon as you get home or lighting up a joint to mellow out, you've been teaching your children that the way to release stress is with drugs.

▼ Do you connect drugs with having a good time? If parties aren't a success unless plenty of booze is at hand, if you think the way to finish a good meal is with a smoke, if you celebrate a raise by scoring some coke, you've taught your kids that the way to have fun is with drugs.

▼ Do you keep a collection of pills handy for your health? Virtually everyone requires some prescription medication as they grow older, but careful parents take only as much as they require and throw out old pills as soon as the problem is gone. Parents who unnecessarily numb themselves with constant use of tranquilizers, hop from doctor to doctor to pick up barbiturates, rely on amphetamines for dieting or even keep a cabinet overflowing with every over-the-counter medication sold by the neighborhood pharmacy train their kids that drugs are the answer whenever they feel bad. A "pill for every ill" is a prescription for drug abuse.

Parents who want to be credible when they sit down with their kids for that crucial series of drug talks should place sensible limits on their own use of alcohol and other drugs—or better yet, stop all use except that necessary to health. Whenever possible, make this shift in the family atmosphere first. Parents should never make a deal to cut down on their own drug use to get their kids to stop using drugs. Parents set rules, they don't make deals.

A note on parents with drug-dependency problems: Nobody knows the number of adult alcoholics in this country, although most estimates put their total in the millions. Millions more Americans are addicted to illicit drugs. And tens of millions are so addicted to nicotine that they can't give up smoking. Obviously, many millions of those dependent on drugs are also parents. The children of dependent parents are far more likely to become dependent themselves.

When one or both parents are dependent on drugs, there can be no thought of creating a family atmosphere in which drugs are not empha- sized. Such households may be seen as dysfunctional from the outside, but the children in the family don't know any other life and so come to view drug use as normal. Children who see a parent keep a job, a home, a family, even while abusing drugs, get the message that they too can do drugs and keep their lives going.

Children's drug dependency can only occur in a family in which denial and enabling occur. Denial and enabling is the way of life in families in which the parents abuse drugs themselves. Enabling, remember, protects addicts from the consequences of their drug use.

Nothing of what we suggest in this chapter will work unless the dependent parent is forced to face up to his or her addiction. Sometimes the shock of a child on drugs will do this; sometimes the added problems of an addicted child makes family enabling so difficult that it can't go on. We can only hope that someone in a family with both an adult and child on drugs will see this crisis as an opportunity and use it to get help for all. Both national and local support groups are present in virtually every community (see Appendix p. 138). They are invaluable for those living with addicts. Search out the ones in your community and go to a meeting as soon as possible.

Intervening

You've come all this way with us. You've carefully read through all the Red Flags and decided that your child is showing enough of them that drugs

Parents Should:

▼ Learn about drugs themselves.
▼ Learn to recognize the Red Flags that indicate drug use.
▼ Take a definite stand against any form of drug use.
▼ Be proper role models: Ask your children to live as you do, not just as you say.
▼ Build strong family relationships by openly encouraging children to talk freely about problems, drugs, school and work.
▼ Set guidelines and rules that must be followed.
▼ Encourage participation in activities that are constructive, challenging and interesting.
▼ Encourage and help build self-esteem, independence, responsibility and other positive qualities in your children.
▼ Take responsibility for your own children and be concerned for the welfare of others.
▼ Join one of the many parent support groups in your area. (Talk to your school's guidance counselors, members of the clergy or local health professionals if you're not sure how to contact these groups.)
▼ Get to know your neighbors and the parents of your children's friends.
▼ Encourage your children to bring their friends home.
▼ Be a good listener for your children.

Parents Should Not:

- ▼ Accept getting drunk or high as normal.
- ▼ Serve alcohol to children under the legal drinking age.
- ▼ Offer cigarettes or other tobacco to children too young to smoke.
- ▼ Allow areas in the home to be off limits to you.
- ▼ Sponsor or condone activities you or your children are unable to control, such as the unsupervised use of homes.
- ▼ Confront children when they are drunk or high.
- ▼ Threaten, scream or overreact.
- ▼ Blame or make excuses for the child abusing alcohol or other drugs.
- ▼ Expect law enforcement officers or school personnel to raise your children and guide them in life.
- ▼ Be discouraged if your first course of action doesn't work. (Let your children know that you are not giving up and will go to great lengths to ensure that your rules and conditions will be obeyed.)
- ▼ Give up and accept your child as a loser. There are no hopeless cases.

---

are the likely cause. You have no choice but to confront the child now. What do you say? How do you act?

The very worst way is for one parent to hold a screaming confrontation with a child who is drunk or high on drugs. Proper intervention requires planning and preparation. In the same way that we've spent 11 chapters getting you prepared for this moment, you must make sure that you're entirely ready for the confrontation before you ever sit down with your child.

In the following pages we lay out a multistep process that all parents should keep in mind when confronting a child about drugs. Although our process is intended to deal with children on drugs, from those just showing a few Red Flags to addicts who will require immediate inpatient treatment, parents can adapt pieces of it for talks with children who show no Red Flags at all. As we've said, we encourage parents to sit down and talk with their children about drugs regularly and start long before the first Red Flags of drug use become apparent. Guidelines for these talks appear at the end of this chapter.

1. **Create a united front.** Both parents must be prepared to confront their child. Sit down and talk with each other about what you want to say and how you will need to act. If there are other adults or authority figures in the family, make them a part of this discussion. Children have to understand that their family has rules about drug use and that if they

125

are breaking the rules there will be no appeal to another adult, no playing one parent off against another.

Parents who are living apart should still confront their child together; when there is joint custody, the rules must be the same in both households. Even if only one parent is available, emphasize that a family with family rules that the child is breaking still exists. Whatever you say, make sure that you have a single agenda, agreed on by all parties. Then stick to it.

2. **Determine the stage of use.** A child with a heavy drug problem can't be treated in the same way as one who's been caught getting drunk for the first time. Refer to the stages in Chapter 2 and to the Red Flags in Chapters 7–11 to estimate how much of a drug problem you will be facing when you confront your child. Experienced users will have more elaborate defenses and will require different treatment from those in earlier stages.

3. **Talk with others.** Teachers, relatives, friends, neighbors and church leaders all see your child more objectively than you do. They may have additional evidence of drug use or they may know of other problems your child has that you're not aware of. Talking to other adults before you talk to your child gives you a chance to rehearse and reinforce your evidence.

4. **Decide on a goal.** What is it that you're trying to accomplish? Is all you want an admission of drug use and a promise never to do it again? Have you and your spouse agreed on what appropriate punishments—not seeing certain friends, parties off limits, household chores, better grades—might be? Do you need to get your child to agree to an evaluation by a physician or drug professional? Is a treatment program required? Knowing your goals ahead of time will help you to keep the session on course and steer it toward your desired end—and not that of your child's.

5. **Identify likely defenses.** You have to know your child to be able to confront the user inside. Will your child simply deny any accusations, lapse into sullen silence, become enraged, blame others? Decide ahead of time how you will overcome these defenses and what you need to do to ensure that your child understands your message and changes his or her behavior.

6. **Consider the effects on your other children**. Having a child on drugs disrupts the entire family. The extra attention needed by the drug-using child means that parents have less time and energy for their other children, and this may translate into what those other children see as a lack of affection as well. Children whose siblings use drugs are more likely to do drugs themselves.

    Even if they keep from trying drugs, they will need to build defenses to survive in a household focused on another child. These defenses take a variety of forms. Some children respond by turning into near-perfect "superkids." Others passively withdraw, so as to attract the least notice. Still others will force notice on themselves by becoming a clown or a rebel. Make your other kids a part of a family solution by lavishing equal attention and affection on them, and give them roles and responsibilities of their own so that they don't imitate or enable their brother or sister on drugs.

7. **If you've failed before, determine what your mistakes were.** Sadly but realistically, one intervention is usually not enough to get a child permanently off drugs. If you have intervened before and failed, you need to examine your past behaviors to make sure you haven't been inadvertently providing outs for your child. Is the child at a more advanced stage than you thought? Did one parent ease up on agreed-on punishments? Did you accept lies and excuses instead of the truth?

    Parents are not to blame if their child continues to use drugs—that is the child's decision and the child's error. But intervention is like any other new skill: The first time is the hardest and the time when you are most likely to make mistakes. Try to learn from these mistakes instead of letting them defeat you. Never get discouraged and never give up on your child.

    You are now ready to talk to your child. When, where and how you do this will help determine your success.

8. **Set the time aside.** Nothing is as important as talking to your child about drugs. Don't put the confrontation off because of other business. Don't hurry through a session just so you can make a dinner appointment or the start of a movie. Pick out a block of time that you can dedicate to your child. Make sure your child is aware of the importance of the lesson, and don't accept any excuses for him or her not to attend. Whether you announce ahead of time that this will be a talk on drugs depends on your knowledge of your child. Usually being honest and

upfront about the subject is best, but the surprise of being found out may give better results.

9. **Talk to your child only when he or she is not high**. What could possibly be more futile than trying to talk sense to a child who is too drunk or stoned to think? Yet many parents think that Saturday night after their child staggers home from a party is the time to lay down the law. Not only won't drug users remember what has been said, but they are also far more likely to become hostile or violent if confronted while on drugs.

   For late-stage users, finding a time when the child isn't on drugs may be a problem. Mornings, before the drinking or drug taking can start anew, may be the best time for confrontation in these cases.

10. **Be specific about problems and your evidence.** Lay out all the Red Flags you've noticed and explain why you think they are evidence of drug use. If you have proof of drugs, make sure your child knows that. It's best if the child sees that there is no chance of wriggling out of the charge by denial.

    Parents will have to wrestle with the issue of invading their child's privacy, say by searching his or her room. Some parents feel this would be a violation of trust; others feel that by using drugs and possibly keeping illicit drugs in their house, the child has already violated that trust. One way to compromise would be to go through the room unannounced, but with the child present.

11. **Talk with, not at, your child.** Kids on drugs are going to be rebellious and resentful of authority. They may become defensive if accused, hostile if lectured. Emphasize your feelings about drug use. Say, "I feel angry and upset about your drug use." Your feelings are your property and they can't be disputed. Accusations like "why are you doing this to us?" will be seized upon and thrown back in your face. If you listen carefully to what your child says rather than merely yelling and punishing, you may learn about problems you weren't aware of and will need to help solve before the drugs can finally go away.

12. **Set rules and punishments appropriate to the age of the child.** Any rules and punishments you lay down should have two objectives in mind: making the child understand that drugs are wrong and keeping the child away from drugs in the future. Younger children may require no more than a stern lecture. Older kids may demand a combination of rules—

coming home immediately from school, an end to unsupervised parties, a restriction in allowance, a curfew. You need to do whatever is necessary to reclaim your control over your child's life.

If you've already found drugs, set punishments immediately. Kids need to understand that drug use will leave them open to instant discipline. Any other behavior makes you an enabler.

13. Make no deals. Kids who have been flouting family rules with their drug use are going to keep on testing you even after being called on it. They may try to bargain, giving up illicit drugs for alcohol or asking for the right to party on weekends. Don't give in. There is no time that drugs are okay. There is no amount of drugs that is okay.

Drugs can be either psychologically or physically addictive or both. Children in the later stages of drug use have progressed beyond the point where a simple "go to your room" style of punishment will work. Any child who has progressed beyond late Stage 2 or early Stage 3 needs to be professionally evaluated and will probably require either an outpatient or inpatient treatment program.

14. Select a treatment program that views drug addiction as a primary disease. Drug addiction is a disease. Although many troubled youth on drugs have emotional or physical problems that are bound up with their drug taking, getting your child off drugs is the first crucial step. All the other problems will be easier to treat when your child is drug-free.

15. Look for the best treatment programs. The best programs: have measurable goals for success; emphasize drug education for the patient; emphasize group counseling; have staff expert in addiction treatment; use abstinence as the criterion for a successful treatment; involve parents in the child's treatment and education; and have good aftercare programs. Visit these programs if possible. Talk with the staff. Ask questions about how they evaluate their patients, what they consider to be a successful outcome, how they involve parents in aftercare. Make sure they consider drugs the primary disease they are treating. Not all programs are equal. If one doesn't work, another may succeed later on.

16. Give your child all the support he or she needs. Children on drugs are difficult to live with, and a confrontation is not going to be a magical solution to all problems. A certain percentage of children will continue to use drugs or relapse back into their use even after a confrontation.

Some of these children are testing you to see if you will really give the support you promised, if punishments will be firm but fair, whether you will join support programs. Since you will have all the old problems plus the hostility and tension arising from the confrontation, your patience and discipline will be sorely tried.

Even a completely drug-free child needs continual support to make it through the first weeks and months of being clean. You can't ask someone to give up their friends (since these are usually also drug users), agree they have made numerous mistakes and admit they are addicted or have the disease of drugs, and then ask them to start all over again while sending them off alone. It won't work. Few true addicts get entirely clean the first time they quit drugs. Most take several sessions. Once again: Never give up.

17. Get others involved. Being supportive and loving parents isn't enough. You can't be at your child's side 24 hours a day. And the addict needs to know that wherever he or she goes, others will be there if the need arises. Tim has a story to tell that, even though it's about an older youth, makes this point strongly:

> As I was giving a talk to a parent's group on the importance of support, I noticed an older lady in the back of the room crying the whole time. She came up afterward to apologize and had a story of her own to tell.
>
> She first caught her son smoking cigarettes at the age of 14. As time went on he got involved with marijuana, alcohol and other drugs. He went through the normal progression of high school, sports and work, but as he got older his drug and alcohol use got worse. By the time he was in his mid-twenties he was having numerous drug-related disorders: blackouts, violence, personality problems, job problems. His mother, his girlfriend and others all acted as enablers for him when he came home drunk and high. He'd break things in his mother's house and the next day cry and apologize for what he did the night before. He would tell his mom it would never happen again, but that never came true.
>
> Finally his mother convinced him to seek professional help. She said she would go with him, and she did. Things were improving until she had to go to the hospital for an operation. She was bedridden for quite some time afterward and not able to go to the treatment and support programs with her son. The son asked everyone he knew to go with him—family, friends, co-workers—but no one had the time. So he stopped going, although his mother never knew this because he lied to her to keep her happy.
>
> Then one day he pulled his car into the garage, left the motor running, pulled

the garage door down and left his mom a loving farewell note. In it he said how much he loved his mother, girlfriend and family, but was so ashamed of his miserable and non-productive life that he thought he should end it. The funeral home was packed with friends, football buddies from high school, relatives, neighbors.

When the mother told me that story she asked me to ask everyone one simple question—"Where the hell were you when my son needed you most?"

The Aftermath: Creating a Drug-Free House

Confrontation, treatment, even support—none of it is enough if you're just going to let your children wander back into a life that is filled with drugs. You may not be able to empty the world of drugs, but you have the power to make your house a drug-free zone for your children. We've already talked about the need for adjusting your own attitudes toward drugs. Following are a few other common-sense rules that all parents should make a part of their everyday lives.

1. **Communicate values openly**. Parents set the values in their household. They may do it by example—either good or bad—but it's best if they openly tell their children what it is they believe in. We'll provide some guidelines for what to say about drugs in the following pages, but parents shouldn't let it stop there. Your children should hear you talk about honesty, responsibility and how to make the correct decision from an early age. And be sure to practice what you preach.

2. **Set rules that are specific, consistent and reasonable.** Children who use drugs should know without question that they are going to be punished. If you as parents have been talking with them as they grow, they should already understand the reasons for these rules; if not, sit down with them now and do so. Use family discussions to allow your children to be a part of setting the rules and appropriate punishments. Not only does this help them to learn responsibility, but they also can't later call the punishment unfair when rules are broken. Family rules should hold for all occasions and situations: in your home, at friends' houses, at parties. Carry out the punishment exactly as stated, and then make sure the child knows that you'll be even stricter the next time.

3. **Keep drugs in the home to an absolute minimum.** Remove temptation from your children's paths. Lock up any alcohol you keep for your own use. Clear the beer out of the refrigerator and the wine out of the wine rack.

   Never keep any prescription medications lying around unless they are currently needed: Old pill bottles provide a temptation to youngsters looking for an easy high. Clean out your medicine cabinet. Even non-prescription products found in any pharmacy or supermarket—especially alcohol-laced cough medicines, sleeping pills, caffeine pills and diet pills—are easily abused by youth.

4. **Allow no illicit drug use by anyone.** It should go without saying that any adult who keeps illicit drugs in the home is sending a clear message that drug use is okay. Whatever your feelings about the legalization or decriminalization of drugs, you can't get your kids to obey the law while they watch you break it.

   Parents shouldn't stop there, however. You need to go one step further and treat alcohol and tobacco as equally taboo. Remember that for others to sell your kids either one is a crime. Sharing alcohol and tobacco with your kids or allowing them to use it in the house are also crimes against your children.

5. **Monitor your children's activities.** Excessive unsupervised time means time to sneak off and do drugs, time to get so bored that drugs look like a better option, time to get involved with others who are into drugs. Parents don't have to be physically with their children every minute. Instead, work with your children to set up activity schedules and goals for the constructive use of their days. Kids with known drug problems may require an actual written schedule agreed to by both the kids and parents in advance. And then, of course, make sure that they keep to their schedule and that they know the punishments for not doing so.

6. **Work with other parents.** Keeping a single house as a no-drug enclave in a do-drug world is hard. Other parents are having to face similar drug problems with their kids. Talk to them. Try to make your entire block or neighborhood or school as drug-free as possible. Get to know the parents of your child's friends. Every house that helps out is one less place where your kids can easily find drugs. Help organize alcohol- and drug-free dances at your school or work with scout troops to get the anti-drug message across. Communities have more clout than couples. Kids can

also then find support from others in their communities to help them stay off drugs once they've quit, either to supplement their parents' efforts or as a substitute if their parents aren't available.

7. **Be for *a healthy life, not just* against *drugs*.** People who work toward a positive goal work harder than those who are trying not to do something. Make your goal a healthy life, a together family, an upbeat outlook. Emphasize what's gone right rather than nagging, accusing or screaming at kids for what they've done wrong. Tim did this in his home:

> I sat down one day and wrote all the negative and positive things I heard or read in that day. My negative column was very long and my positive column was only a couple of lines. At supper that day I started a new tradition in my house. We say our prayers and then I have each of my three kids say something positive. It can be anything except talking about the food we are eating. My kids say things like, "I am glad my friend came over," "I love my mommy and daddy," "I had fun at school."
>
> The first two days my kids resisted, but after that they really took off with it and it has remained a tradition ever since. When our friends, parents or relatives visit, we include them. The key is that everyone says something positive, mom and dad included. I noticed that because their parents participate the kids are more eager to take part. They're very interested in what we have to say. I believe it will make an impression on how they look at and deal with the many facets of life.

8. **Trust *in your gut feelings*.** These are your kids. You know them better than anyone else in the world. If you think they're starting drugs or are back on drugs, don't hesitate to translate those feelings into action. Let Tim have the last word:

> I truly believe that God has given parents a gift of gut feelings that they should never ignore. When drugs and alcohol are involved, your gut feelings will surface. I have talked to thousands of parents who are trying to figure out what is going on with their child. After talking about the many different clues and personality changes I always ask, "What is your gut feeling?" Parents are like anyone else. They want to know for sure but they want someone else to say, "Yes, your kid is using drugs." Many times I can see that look on their faces and I know that their gut feelings are guiding them in the right direction. Seek out a problem if it exists and be relentless in solving it.

When a Child Is Going Out, Parents Should:

▼ Know where the child is going, and be sure he or she is aware of where you will be.

▼ Establish a time for the child to be home and *demand* to be notified and told why if this curfew is broken.

▼ Be awake when the child comes home at night.

▼ Assure the child that he or she can call to be picked up whenever needed—no questions asked.

▼ Contact parents in charge of an activity to verify the activity and that adequate adult supervision will be provided.

When a Child Is Hosting a Party, Parents Should:

▼ Set up ground rules with the child, such as time span, number of guests, location of party, food, beverages and no alcohol or drugs.

▼ Keep parties small and controllable.

▼ Provide adequate food and entertainment.

▼ Encourage "by invitation only" activities.

▼ Determine how party crashers will be handled.

▼ Prevent guests who leave from returning.

▼ Determine how to deal with guests possessing alcohol or other drugs, or guests under the influence of any drug.

▼ Never allow anyone under the influence of a drug to drive or go home alone.

▼ Be visible and available, but keep a low profile.

▼ Invite another parent or couple to assist in the supervision and act as company for the hosting adults.

Growing Up: Raising a Drug-Free Child

Preschoolers

Start by teaching your children why they should put only good things into their bodies. Explain why good food and wholesome eating habits will allow them to grow strong and healthy. Point out poisonous and dangerous products around the house, such as bleach or furniture polish, and get your children into the habit of reading warning labels. Teach your children never to take anything from a medicine bottle by themselves. And keep all such products out of their reach.

Even at this early age you can provide guidelines that teach your children what behaviors you expect. Educate them to play fair, tell the truth and treat others the way you want them to treat you.

Kindergarten to Grade 3

Discussions about alcohol and other drugs should be specific and focused on the here and now. Most children are very interested in knowing how their bodies work. Focus discussions on how to maintain good health and how to avoid things that might harm their bodies. For example, contrast healthful activities such as brushing teeth, washing hands and getting plenty of rest and sleep against smoking, drinking or taking drugs. Help your children understand the differences between medicines they take when they're sick—which can help them stay healthy—and drugs that can only make them sick.

By the end of the third grade, your children should understand:

▼ What illicit drugs are, why they are illegal, what they look like and what harm they can do.
▼ What the rules are at home and at school about alcohol and other drug use.
▼ Why it is important to avoid unknown and possibly dangerous objects, containers and substances.

Grades 4 to 6

Friends become very important at this age. Many children are "followers," and their self-image is determined in part by the extent to which they are accepted by peers, especially popular ones. Although children this age love learning facts and how things work, what their interests are may be determined by what the group thinks.

Getting your children to be independent and able to say no to others is crucial. These are years of great risk for early drug experimentation, and the earlier youngsters begin to smoke, drink and use other drugs, the more likely they are to develop lasting and serious drug habits.

By the end of the sixth grade, your children should know:

▼ To ask questions about a party or gathering where they suspect drugs might be present.

▼ To be able to give reasons for not using drugs, suggest other activities where drugs won't be involved or just leave if there's no other way to avoid a drug situation.
▼ How to identify specific drugs when they see them.
▼ The long- and short-term effects and consequences of drug use.
▼ The effects of drugs on different parts of the body, especially on growing bodies.
▼ The consequences of alcohol and illicit drug use to the user and on family and society.

Grades 7 to 9

By the end of the ninth grade, more than half of all youth have tried drugs. Largely because so many of their friends are trying them, drugs are often part of a new and rebellious life-style. Kids will do this even though this is the age at which they are beginning to appreciate that their actions have consequences and their behavior affects others.

Parents should counteract peer influence with parent influence. Rules against the use of drugs need to be reinforced. Working with the parents of your children's friends is a good way to make sure that all the kids your children play with are getting the same message.

Youth of this age require supervised freedom: Parents should monitor their children's activities and know where they are and with whom. In addition, parents should let their children participate in a periodic review and updating of family rules and responsibilities, to adjust them as appropriate for your children's newfound maturity and responsibility.

The rule prohibiting any alcohol or other drug use has to stay, however. Kids with more independence also have more temptations, and youth who spend more time with their peers become even more concerned about how others see them. Their new, more active lives will make it harder for them to continue to always say no. They'll need your help. Practice ways of saying no with your children. Make up situations in which your children may be asked to try alcohol or other drugs and let your children decide how best to refuse.

By the end of the ninth grade your child should know:

▼ The stages of drug dependency.
▼ How drugs affect the circulatory, respiratory, nervous and reproductive systems.
▼ The ways that drug use affects activities requiring motor coordination, such as driving a car or participating in sports.

▼ Your family's history, particularly if alcoholism or other drug addiction has been a problem.

Grades 10 to 12

While with younger children you may want to emphasize short-term unpleasant effects of drugs—bad breath, stained fingers and teeth, headaches and hangovers—high school students are old enough to start appreciating the long-term problems drugs bring. Older teens can be swayed with the realization that drugs can keep them out of college or the military, leave them with a permanent criminal record, prevent them from getting hired at many firms and ruin their health. Children with younger brothers and sisters may be impressed by the importance of serving as a good role model.

Young adults may long for complete independence, but it is particularly important to keep them involved in family activities. They should join the rest of the family at dinner, be part of family vacations and have their own chores and responsibilities.

By the end of high school, your children should understand:

▼ Both the immediate and long-term physical effects of specific drugs.
▼ The possibly fatal effects of combining drugs.
▼ The relationship of drug use to other diseases and disabilities.
▼ The effects of alcohol and other drugs on the fetus during pregnancy.
▼ The fact that drug use is not a victimless crime.
▼ The effects and possible consequences of operating vehicles or other equipment after having used alcohol or other drugs.
▼ The impact that drug use has on society.
▼ The extent and availability of community intervention resources.

These guidelines are adapted from *Growing Up Drug-Free: A Parent's Guide to Prevention*, a U.S. Department of Education (DOE) publication. Copies of the free guide, which we highly recommend, are available by calling the DOE's toll-free number, 1- 800-624-0100. They are also available by writing to Growing Up Drug Free, Pueblo, CO 81009, or the National Clearinghouse for Alcohol and Drug Information, P.O. Box 2345, Rockville, MD 20852.

Appendix

National Organizations Dealing with Alcohol and Other Drug Abuse

Parents have thousands of national, state and local organizations to turn to no matter what their needs are. Following is a list of some of the better-known national organizations, from which a variety of information on drugs and youth is available. You can get the address of your nearest local chapter directly from these national headquarters or from listings in local phone books.

Every state also has an office dealing with alcoholism and drug abuse from which additional information can be obtained. These go under many names but should be in the phone book under the state heading.

Well-run and helpful local groups can be found everywhere in the country, even in communities without branches of these national organizations.

Parents should investigate all groups, asking for references and credentials of employees. Books are available to help you choose from among the many treatment centers in the country. The most comprehensive listing of such centers is in *Drug, Alcohol, and other Addictions: A Directory of Treatment Centers and Prevention Programs Nationwide*, published in 1989 by the Oryx Press, 2214 North Central at Encanto, Phoenix, AZ 85004. It should be available at most large public libraries.

Groups that use the 12-step method made famous by Alcoholics Anonymous or the "tough-love" approach originated by the Palmer Drug Abuse Program, however, are using systems that have been proven to work for many thousands of youth suffering from problems with drugs.

Al-Anon Family Group
  Headquarters
P.O. Box 862
Midtown Station
New York, NY 10018

Alcohol, Drug Abuse and Mental
  Health Administration
Department of Health and Human
  Services
5600 Fishers Lane, Room 6C15
Rockville, MD 20857
301-443-4797

Alcoholics Anonymous World
Services
P.O. Box 459
Grand Central Station
212-686-1100

Cocaine Anonymous World—
Services
3740 Overland Avenue, Suite G
Los Angeles, CA 90034
213-559-5833

Drugs Anonymous
P.O. Box 473
Ansonia Station
New York, NY 10023
212-874-0700

Families Anonymous
P.O. Box 528
Van Nuys, CA 94108
818-989-7841

Families in Action National Drug
Information Center
2296 Henderson Mill Road, Suite
204
Atlanta, GA 30345
404-934-6364

Friendly Persuasion
c/o Girls' Incorporated
441 W. Michigan Street
Indianapolis, IN 46202
317-634-7546

Group Against Smokers' Pollution
(GASP)

P.O. Box 632
College Park, MD 20740
301-459-4791

Indian Health Services (IHS)
Alcohol and Substance Program
5600 Fishers Lane, Room 38
Rockville, MD 20857
301-443-4297

Institute on Black Chemical
Abuse
2616 Nicollet Avenue S.
Minneapolis, MN 55408
612-871-7878

Mothers Against Drunk Driving
(MADD)
511 E. John Carpenter Freeway No.
700
Irving, TX 75062
214-744-6233

Narcotics Anonymous
P.O. Box 9999
Van Nuys, CA 91049
818-780-3951

National Asian Pacific American
Families Against Substance
Abuse
6303 Friendship Court
Bethesda, Maryland 20817
301-530-0945

National Association for
Children of Alcoholics
31582 Coast Highway, Suite B
South Laguna, CA 92677
714-499-3889

Appendix

National Black Alcoholism
    Council
1629 K St. NW, Suite 802
Washington, D.C. 20006
202-296-2696

National Clearinghouse for Drug
    Abuse Information
Department of Healthe and
    Human Services
5600 Fishers Lane, Room 10A53,
P.O. Box 2345
Rockville, MD 10857
301-443-6500

National Federation of Parents
    for Drug-Free Youth
1423 N. Jefferson
Springfield, MO 65802
417-836-3709

National Hispanic Family Against
    Drugs
1511 K Street, NW
Washington, D.C. 20005
202-393-5136

National Parents' Resource
    Institute for Drug Education
    (PRIDE)
50 Hurt Plaza, Suite 210
Atlanta, GA 30303
404-577-4500

Parent Resources and Information
    on Drug Education
Georgia State University
University Plaza
Atlanta, GA 30303
404-658-2548

Pil-Anon Family Program
P.O. Box 120
Gracie Square Station
New York, NY 10028
212-744-2020

Pills Anonymous
P.O. Box 473
Ansonia Station
New York, NY 10023
212-375-8872

Potsmokers Anonymous
316 East 3rd Street
New York, NY 10009
212-254-1777

Secular Organizations for
    Sobriety (SOS)
National Clearinghouse
Box 5
Buffalo, NY 14215
Tel (716) 834-2921

Stop Teen-Age Addiction to
    Tobacco (STAT)
121 Lyman St., Suite 210
Springfield, MA 01103
413-732-STAT

Straight, Inc.
3001 Gandy Boulevard
St. Petersburg, FL 33702
813-576-8929

Students Against Driving Drunk
    (SADD)
P.O. Box 800
Marlboro, MA 01752
508-481-3568

Toughlove, International
P.O. Box 1069
Doylestown, PA 18901
215-348-7090

Valium Anonymous
P.O. Box 404
Altoona, IA 50009
515-967-6781

Women for Sobriety
P.O. Box 618
Quakertown, PA 18951
215-536-8026

Further Reading

Addeo, Edmond G. and Jovita Reichling Addeo, *Why Our Children Drink.* Englewood Cliffs, N.J.: Prentice-Hall, 1975.

Allinson, Russel R., *Drug Abuse: Why It Happens and How to Prevent It.* Lower Burrell, Penn.: Valley Publications, 1983, 1984.

Barun, Ken and Philip Bashe, *How to Keep the Children You Love Off Drugs.* New York: Atlantic Monthly Press, 1988.

Duncan, David and Robert Gold, *Drugs and the Whole Person.* New York: John Wiley & Sons, 1982.

DuPont, Robert L. Jr., *Getting Tough on Gateway Drugs.* Washington D.C.: American Psychiatric Press, 1984.

Freeman, Jodi, *How to Drug-Proof Kids: A Parents' Guide to Early Prevention.* Albuquerque, N.M.: Think Shop, 1989.

Harrity, Anne Swany and Ann Bley Christensen, *Kids, Drugs, and Alcohol: A Parent's Guide to Prevention and Intervention.* Crozet, Virginia: Betterway Publications, 1987.

Jabobs, Michael and Kevin O'B. Fehr, *Drugs and Drug Abuse: A Reference Text,* second edition, revised. Toronto: Addiction Research Foundation, 1987.

Macdonald, Donald Ian, *Drugs, Drinking, and Adolescents.* Chicago: Year Book Medical Publishers, 1984.

Miller, Angelyn, *The Enabler: When Helping Harms the Ones You Love.* Claremont, Calif.: Hunter House, 1988.

Neff, Pauline, *Tough Love: How Parents Can Deal With Drug Abuse.* Nashville: Abingson Press, 1982.

Polson, Beth and Miller Newton, *Not My Kid: A Parents' Guide to Kids and Drugs.* New York: Arbor House, 1984.

Rogers, Ronald L. and Chandler Scott McMillin, *Freeing Someone You Love from Alcohol and Other Drugs.* Los Angeles: Price, Stern, Sloan, 1989.

Further Reading

Ryan, Elizabeth A., *Straight Talk About Drugs and Alcohol*. New York: Facts On File, 1989.

Stacy, Nita C., ed., *Americans for a Drug-Free America*. Austin, Texas: American Crisis Publishing, 1988.

United States Department of Education, *Growing Up Drug Free: A Parent's Guide to Prevention*. Washington, D.C.: U.S. Department of Education, n.d.

United States Department of Education, *What Works: Schools Without Drugs*. Washington, D.C.: U.S. Department of Education, 1986.

Van Ost, William C. and Elaine Van Ost, *Warning Signs: A Parent's Guide to In-Time Intervention in Drug and Alcohol Abuse*. New York: Warner, 1988.

York, Phyllis and David and Ted Wachtel, *Toughlove: A Self-Help Manual for Parents Troubled by Teenage Behavior*. Sellersville, Penn.: Community Service Foundation, 1980.

Youcha, Geraldine and Judith S. Seixas, *Drugs, Alcohol, and Your Children*. New York: Crown, 1989.

The Michigan Survey, referred to in Chapter 1, is an annual survey of high school seniors and other youth to determine their use of and attitudes toward drugs and drug use. It is sometimes referred to simply as the High School Senior Survey, even though representative samples of young adults from previous graduating classes are also surveyed. The entire research project is entitled "Monitoring the Future: A Continuing Study of the Lifestyles and Values of Youth," and is conducted by the University of Michigan's Institute for Social Research and funded by the National Institute on Drug Abuse.

A variety of reports, summaries and studies are issued either annually or individually. Unfortunately, a different title is given to each annual volume, although all have been authored by Lloyd D. Johnston, Patrick M. O'Malley and Jerald G. Bachman. The last annual volume generally available in book form is the one issued in 1989, *Drug Use, Drinking, and Smoking: National Survey Results from the High School, College, and Young Adult Populations, 1975–1988*. More recent survey results may be found in the government documents section of those large public or university libraries that act as government depositories, or from the United States Superintendent of Documents, U.S. Government Printing Office, Washington, D.C. 20402.

Index of Signs and Symptoms of Drug Use

Index

Head nodding, 47
Headaches, 33, 39, 104
Heart rate: decreased, 47; increased, 36, 39, 40,
    42, 44, 45, 50
Heartbeat, irregular 33, 39, 47
Hopelessness, 86
Hunger, 39
Hyperactivity, 40, 110–11

Illness, frequent, 104
Impotence, 33, 39
Incense, use of, 98
Incoherence, 45, 106
Initiative, loss of, 85
Injection marks, 47, 109–110
Insomnia, 35, 39, 40, 50
Instant gratification, need for, 83
Intoxication, 34

Jamming (from LSD use), 43, 44, 111
Jaundice, 50, 109–110
Job-related problems, 101–102
Judgment, impaired, 33, 36, 43

Kegs, 33

Lateness, 88, 93
Legal problems, 119–121
Light, sensitivity to, 35, 36
Lighters, 114
Lips: dry, 108–109, 117; moisturizers, 117
Liquids, 42, 43, 45, 47
Lock box, 98, 99
Loneliness, 58
Lying, 67–68, 87

Maturity, lack of, 83
Memory loss, 33, 34, 43, 45, 106–107
Menstruation, irregular, 50, 105
Mood swings, 33, 34, 35, 39, 47, 82
Motor control, loss of, 33, 34, 110–111
Mouth, dry. See Dry mouth
Munchies, the, 42, 96
Muscle mass, sudden growth of, 50, 105
Muscle weakness, 34, 36, 110–111
Mushrooms, 43

Nasal spray, 117
Nausea, 33, 34, 36, 44, 45, 47, 48
Needles, 116–117
Nightmares, 35
Nosebleeds, 36, 108. See also Runny nose
Numbness, 36

Occult, interest in, 97–98
Odors from solvents, 36. See also
    Smells

Pallor, 39
Panic, 35, 43, 44, 45
Paper bags, 35, 116
Paranoia, 40, 41, 42, 44, 45, 88–89
Paraphernalia, 54, 99, 113–117
Passivity, 85
Personal hygiene, lack of, 86, 96, 111–112
Personality, changes in, 81–91
Physical appearance, changes in, 103–112
Pills, 34, 39, 43, 45, 47
Pipes, 42, 113–14; accessories, 114
Plastic bags, 35, 116
Powders, 39, 43, 44, 45, 46, 47
Profanity, excessive, 98
Prostitution, 24, 95, 119
Pseudohallucinations. See Hallucinations
Pupils: constricted, 35, 45, 47, 107–108; dilated,
    35, 38, 40, 45, 48, 107–108; pinpoint, 47
Rags, 35, 116
Recklessness, 89–90
Religion, loss of interest in, 97–98
Respiration. See Breathing
Roach clips, 116
Rock music, excessive interest in, 99
Roid rage, 50, 89–90
Rolling papers, 114–115
Runny nose, 36, 38, 48, 107

Sadness, 86
Satanism. See Devil-worship
School-related problems, 85, 100–101, 106
Sedation, 34
Self-esteem, low, 58, 86, 90, 112
Selling possessions, 96–97
Sexual relationships, changes in, 50, 84–85, 95,
    105–106
Shoplifting, 118
Skin, 109–110: burning or itching, 47; cold and
    clammy, 34, 47; puffy and tight, 50; rash, 40;
    unexplained darkening of, 50, 109–110
Slang, new, 98
Sleep disturbances, 34, 39, 40, 43, 50, 96
Smell on breath, hair, or clothes, 33,
    42
Sneezing, 36
Sniffles, 38
Speech, slurred, 33, 34, 36, 45, 106
Spots on body, purple or red, 50, 109–110
Stealing, 24, 54, 96–97
Strength and energy, intense feelings of, 40
Stretch marks, pronounced, 50
Stupor, 33, 35, 36, 47
Sugar cubes, 43
Suicide, 33, 45, 91
Sunglasses, 108, 117
Sweating, 33, 40, 43, 44, 45, 47, 48
Swelling, 50

146

Index

Tablets, 39, 44, 47, 50
Talkativeness, 33, 36, 38, 42, 47
Tattoos, 109–110
Temperature, body: increased, 39, 40, 44; low, 35, 47
Testicles, shrinking of, 50
Tremors, 33, 35, 36, 39, 44, 48, 50

Urine output: decreased, 45; increased; 40, 45, 47

Vandalism, 89, 119–120

Vials, 38, 50
Violent behavior, 45, 50, 90
Violent crime, 119–120
Vision, blurred or double, 34, 45, 107–108
Voice, deepening of, 50
Vomiting, 33, 39, 45, 47, 49

Weight loss, 35, 36, 104
Withdrawal, 33, 42, 93
Work-related problems. *See* Job-related problems

Index of
Drugs and Drug Nicknames

Index

Index

General Index

AIDS, from sharing needles, 50, 117
Alcohol. *See* Drugs; Gateway drugs
Alcoholism, genetic component in, 59
Anabolic body changes, from
    steroids, 48
Anabolic Steroid Control Act of 1990, 49
Androgenic body changes, from
    steroids, 48
Athletes, use of steroids by, 48, 55, 73

Bad trips, effects of, 41, 44

Caretaker parent, 65
Celebrities, drug use by, 13, 48, 73–74
Children: curiosity about drugs in, 18; denial
    in, 66–69; experimentation in, 19; guidelines
    for, 134–137; identities, forming in, 57, 134–
    137; imitating parents' drug use, 17–18, 59,
    122–124; numbers of drug users among, 2,
    8–9, 10–13, 14, 23, 32, 38, 41, 46, 49; reasons
    for use of drugs, 52–60; rules for, 128–129,
    131–133, 134; stages of drug use in, 16–28;
    users of drugs, by race, 14; values, commu-
    nicating to, 131–133
Confronting child on drugs, 22, 122, 125–128
Conning behaviors, 21, 63, 67, 87, 97
Crime, and drugs, 24, 26, 56, 96–97, 118–20
Cross-addiction, 31, 77

Denial, 22, 61–69: definition of, 61; parental
    denial, 61–66; user denial, 66–69
Driving, and drugs, 5, 8, 9, 111, 118–119
Dropouts, 10–1, 21
Drug categories, 28–51
Drug use, reasons for, 18, 19, 52–58
Drugs: advertisements for, 59–60;
    appearance, 29, 33, 34, 35, 38, 39, 42, 43–44,
    45, 46–47, 50; children's attitudes toward,
    11–12; combinations of, 7, 17, 23, 31, 38, 39,
    41, 42, 43, 45, 53; effects of long-term use of,
    30, 33, 34, 36, 39, 40, 43, 44, 45, 47, 50; effects
    of short-term use of, low to moderate dos-
    age, 30, 33, 34, 36, 39, 40, 42, 44, 45, 47, 50;
    effects of short-term use of, high dosage, 30,
    33, 34, 36, 39, 40, 43, 44, 45, 47, 50; history
    of, in America, 3–7; illicit, definition of, 3;
    individual, 31–51; individual, signs of use of,
    30, 33, 34, 36, 38, 40, 42, 44, 45, 47, 50;
    nicknames of, 29–30, 33, 34, 36, 38, 40, 42,
    44, 45, 47, 50; numbers of users of, 2, 8–9,
    10–12, 14, 23, 32, 38, 41, 46, 49, 122, 123;
    overdoses of, 30, 33, 35, 36, 39, 40, 43, 44, 46,
    47, 51; and sex, 24, 55, 95, 119; trade names of,
    29, 33, 34, 36, 38, 39, 42, 44, 45, 47, 50; with-
    drawal symptoms of, 30, 33, 35, 36, 39, 40, 43,
    44, 46, 48, 51

Enabling, 61, 71–74

Families, drug use in, 64–66, 127; drug-free
    household for, 134–138; rules for, 134
Fear, 71–72

Gateway drugs: availability of, 17–18; defini-
    tion of, 3; long-term use of, 19; in the media,
    73; potential dangers of, 9–10; reported use
    of, 121
*Growing-Up Drug-Free: A Parent's Guide to Preven-
    tion*, 137
Guilt, 70–71
Intervention, 22, 25, 27, 69, 124–31

Jobs, and drugs, 24, 26, 101–102

Latchkey kids, 56
Limits, on drug use, 123, 132
Love, 72

Music, 55, 99

Parents: creating drug-free home by, 131–133;
    raising drug-free children, 134–38; responsi-
    bilities of, 15; rules to follow, 124, 125, 134;
    talking to children about drugs, 17, 73; use of
    drugs by, 59, 63–64, 122–124
Parties: drug use in, 20, 55; rules for,
    134
Polyuse. *See* Cross-addiction

Rebellion, in children, 55, 56, 57
Red Flags, as warning signs of drug use: defini-
    tions of, 76–77; individual, 81–120; number
    visible of, 121–122; patterns of, 77–78
Rehabilitation, 22, 27, 57, 129

Second users, 65
Siblings, as drug users, 64–66, 71–72
Single parents, 56
Society, drug messages in, 59, 73–74

Index

152